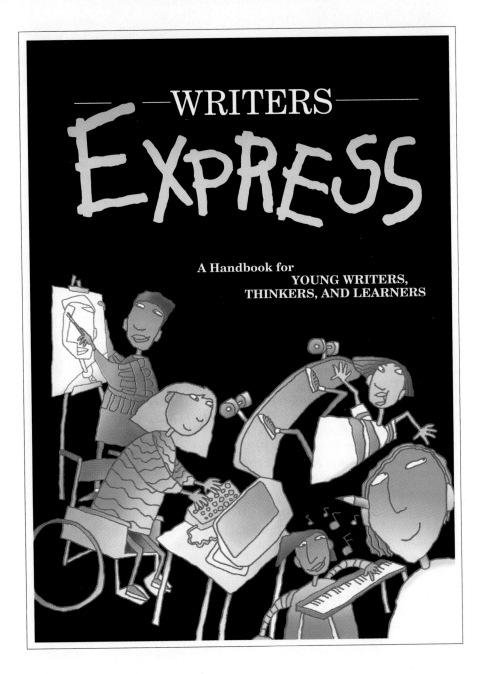

# WRITERS EXPRESS

A Handbook for **YOUNG WRITERS, THINKERS, AND LEARNERS**

Written and Compiled by
**Dave Kemper, Ruth Nathan, Patrick Sebranek**

Illustrated by Chris Krenzke

## WRITE SOURCE®

GREAT SOURCE EDUCATION GROUP
a Houghton Mifflin Company
Wilmington, Massachusetts

# Acknowledgements

We're grateful to many people who helped bring *Writers Express* to life. First, we must thank all the students from across the country who've contributed their writing and their ideas.

Also, thanks to some of our favorite authors and teachers who helped make *Writers Express* a reality.

**Sandy Asher** for *Writing Realistic Stories* and *Writing Plays*
**Nancy Bond** for *Writing Fantasies*
**Roy Peter Clark** for *Writing Newspaper Stories*
**Will Hobbs** for *Revising Your Writing*
**Toby Fulwiler** for *Writing as a Learning Tool*
**Stephen Krensky** for *Writing Stories from History*
**Gloria Nixon-John** for *Giving Speeches*
**Susan Ohanian** for *Writing Tall Tales*
**Anne-Marie Oomen** for *Writing Poems*
**Marie Ponsot** for *Sharing Family Stories*
**Peter and Connie Roop** for *Writing a Classroom Report*
**Paula and Keith Stanovich** for *Building Vocabulary Skills*
**Lorraine Sintetos** for *Writing Riddles*
**Peter Stillman** for *Writing for Fun*
**Charles Temple** for *Becoming a Better Speller* and *Writing Songs*
**Toni Walters** for *Using Reading Strategies*
**Allan Wolf** for *Performing Poems*

Another thank-you goes to our team of educators, editors, and designers: Laura Bachman, Laurie Cooper, Marguerite Cotto, Carol Elsholz, Tom Gilding, Julie Janosz, Beverly Jessen, Kathy Juntunen, Lois Krenzke, Heather Monkmeyer, Candyce Norvell, Sherry Schenning-Gordon, Ed Schuster, Linda Sivy, and Sandy Wagner.

Printed in the United States of America

International Standard Book Number: 0-669-38633-2 (hardcover) 0-669-38632-4 (softcover)

17 18 19 20 21 -RRDC- 04 03 02 01 00

# Express Yourself!

***Writers Express* is divided into five major parts . . .**

**1** **The Process of Writing** ● Use this section to answer your questions about writing, from selecting a subject to proofreading a final draft.

**2** **The Forms of Writing** ● Would you like to start a personal journal, or write a poem, or create a tall tale? Then this section is for you!

**3** **The Tools of Learning** ● If your study, reading, or test-taking skills could use a little pumping up, turn to "The Tools of Learning."

**4** **The Proofreader's Guide** ● Have a question about punctuation? Spelling? Capitalization? Here's where you can "Check It Out!"

**5** **The Student Almanac** ● Full-color maps, a historical time line, the metric system— *Writers Express* is truly an all-school handbook!

# Table of Contents

# The Process of Writing

# The Forms of Writing

# The Tools of Learning

## Improving Your Reading

## Improving Your Spelling and Vocabulary

## Improving Your Speaking and Listening

## Improving Your Thinking

## Improving Your Learning Skills

# Proofreader's Guide: Check It Out

# The Student Almanac

## Useful Tables and Lists

## Using Maps

## Improving Math Skills

## History in the Making

## Index

# Why Write?

## A Note from the Editors

Not too long ago, in a not too faraway place, a bunch of friends got together during summer vacation and started a newspaper. *King's Cove* they called it, after a park in their neighborhood. Each issue was filled with the local gossip, the latest jokes, lists of stuff for sale, and the names of good books to read. Some writers added stories; others wrote poems. A few wrote basic news reports.

Why did these friends go to all of this trouble and do all of this writing? Why not just hang out and goof around? If you were to ask them, you might be surprised by their answers.

## Summer Fun

First, they'd tell you writing a newspaper was fun! Yes, it was a lot of work; but in school they had a classroom newspaper, and it was just plain fun to see their ideas and names in print.

## Feeling Good

Second, they would tell you it felt terrific working as a team, helping each other out.  And third, they would admit that having the other kids read the newspaper gave them a feeling of pride.  They were **being heard** and **feeling useful**.

Why write?  This group of young writers, in talking about *King's Cove,* offered some very good answers.  They wrote to have fun, to work together, and to be heard.  We could not have said it better ourselves.

> **❝**Writing blows me away! Each time I write, I realize I know more than I thought.  Cool ideas pop up out of nowhere.**❞**
> —Chris, *King's Cove* writer

## The Express Connection

We've created *Writers Express* to help make writing an important part of your life, no matter if you are completing assignments in school or working on writing projects in your own neighborhood.  Many writers, teachers, and students from across the country have helped put this handbook together, and it is loaded with all kinds of great writing ideas.

Always have your copy of *Writers Express* right next to you when you write.  Then turn to it for help whenever you have any questions about your work.

Once you get to know the handbook better, you will see that it is a writing guide plus much more.  It contains information that will help you become a better reader, thinker, speaker, learner, and all-around student.  Not bad for one little book!

> **❝** *Why write?  Maybe we should ask, Why write and read and think and speak and learn?  We hope you find many answers to either question in Writers Express—and we hope that you have a lot of fun along the way.* **❞**
> —The Editors

# The Process of Writing

# Getting Started

**All About Writing**

**One Writer's Process**

**A Basic Writing Guide**

**Writing with a Computer**

**Planning Your Portfolio**

# All About Writing

## Wishful Thinking

Let's say that you plot out your next writing assignment on your special computer pad, like this:

**Subject:** Class elections
**Purpose:** To report on election results
**Form:** News story
**Audience:** Students at Pitts Elementary

Then you plug your keyboard into the pad, set it on automatic pilot, and eat a piece of pizza or read a good book while your story is being written. This would take all of the work and worry out of writing. By pressing a few buttons, your writing would come out just the way you ordered it, every time.

## The Real Story

As you probably know, such a gizmo has not been invented yet. For now, and for years to come, you will have to work very closely with your writing to make sure it is done right. You, and *only you*, are in control of the words and ideas you put on paper. And this is exactly how it should be. Writing is too important to be left in the "hands" of a machine.

# Points to Remember

The ideas listed below will help you understand what writing is really all about.

✔ *Writing is a natural thing to do.*

All of us have the ability to write (even without the help of a special computer pad). This is especially true when you write to learn and to explore your own thoughts and feelings.

✔ *Writing is a lot of different things, and all of them are important.*

Writing is thinking on paper. Writing is learning new things. Writing is making contact with friends and family members. Writing is dealing with bad days, and much more.

*❝I have found another side of myself that I've never known before. When I leave 5th grade, I'm not going to stop writing because I don't want to close up a world that I just unlocked. ❞*

—Heidi Bimschleger, grade 5

✔ *Writing is a process.*

Your favorite writers do a lot of planning, writing, and rewriting to produce the books and stories you like to read. That is why writing is called a process. It's very important for young writers like you to understand and use this process in your own writing. (You will learn more about the writing process on the next pages.)

✔ *Writing is a skill that must be practiced.*

Your handbook says a lot of good things about writing. But there is really only one way to learn how to write, and that is by actually putting pen or pencil to paper, or fingers to the keyboard. That's why it is important to practice all kinds of writing: journal writing, story writing, report writing, and so on. (Even writing notes to friends is good practice.)

# The Steps in the Process

When we talk about the writing process, we really mean the steps a writer usually follows whenever he or she writes. We have divided the writing process into the following basic steps:

**PREWRITING** refers to selecting a subject, collecting details, and any other planning that goes on during a writing project.

**WRITING THE FIRST DRAFT** refers to the actual writing, when a writer gets all of his or her ideas on paper. (Writers often write more than one draft.)

**REVISING** refers to the changes a writer makes to improve his or her writing. Ideas may be added, cut, or switched around; sentences may be cut or rewritten.

**EDITING & PROOFREADING** refers to all of the final changes made in the revised writing. During this step, writing is checked carefully for errors.

**PUBLISHING**

There is one more important step in the process—publishing. Sharing your story with friends or classmates is one form of publishing; so is sending it to the school or city newspaper. You will naturally work harder at your writing if you know that it is going to be published. (**SEE** pages 54-57 for more information.)

**THINK IT OVER**

A writer may repeat some of these steps before a piece of writing is finished. For example, after the first draft, a writer may decide to do some more prewriting and planning.

# The Writing Process in Action

These two pages provide a basic look at the writing process in action. You will find this information helpful if you have never used the writing process before or if you would like a general guide to follow when you write.

## PREWRITING

Prewriting means getting ready to write. Follow these basic steps during prewriting:

■ **Select** a subject that really interests you.

■ **Collect** details about your subject if you don't know a lot about it.

■ **Plan** what you want to say about your subject (the main idea of your writing) and how you want to say it (the form of your writing).

## WRITING THE FIRST DRAFT

Once you've collected your thoughts about your subject, write the first draft of your paper.

■ **Write** this draft freely, getting *all* of your ideas on paper.

■ **Imagine** that you are talking to a group of friends.

■ **Let** your prewriting and planning be your guide as you write.

## REVISING

When you revise, you try to make improvements in your draft. Follow this basic revising plan:

- ■ **Read** your draft two or three times.
- ■ **Ask** at least one classmate or friend to read and react to your draft.
- ■ **Decide** what changes need to be made.
- ■ **Work** on improving your writing.

## EDITING & PROOFREADING

When you edit and proofread, you make sure the revised version of your writing is clear and accurate. Follow this basic editing and proofreading plan:

- ■ **Look** closely at the style of your writing. (Your words and sentences should read smoothly.)
- ■ **Check** your writing for spelling, punctuation, and grammar errors. (Ask for help from a classmate or teacher.)
- ■ **Write or type** a neat final draft of your writing.
- ■ **Proofread** this draft for any additional errors.

# One Writer's Process

## One Step at a Time

For one of her assignments, Hillary Bachman was asked to write about her favorite teacher. Here's how she used the writing process to complete her assignment.

**PREWRITING** *Planning Your Way*

**Selecting a Subject** ● Hillary started by thinking about all of her favorite teachers, past and present. She thought of Mrs. Thompson, Mr. Schwarz, Mrs. Bolstad, and Mr. Vetter. The one teacher that really stood out was Mr. Vetter, so she decided to write about him.

**Collecting Details** ● She then freely listed ideas about her subject.

funny, nice, helpful, coach, two boys my age,
helps students, friend, room 203, math,
fun learning, answers questions, laughs,
tells us jokes, we learn, sees when I'm upset,
called Mr. V, . . .

## WRITING THE FIRST DRAFT

Mr. Vetter was one of Hillary's current teachers, so she had no trouble writing about him.  This is part of her first draft.

**Hillary starts with words from her collecting list.** →

**She continues by writing freely about her subject.** →

A Great Teacher

Funny, helpful, and friendly.  What am I describing?  Is it one of your classmates or your best friend?  Beleive it or not, I'm describing a teacher! His name is Mr. Vetter. We call him Mr. V.

One thing that really like about him is the way he makes learning fun.

If math seams boring, he will make it fun by saying something that is so funny so you want to learn.  Once I sneezed really loud in the middle of class.  Right away, Mr. V. said "googolplex*." It sounded just the same as gesundheit or bless you.

Mr. V. also...

*Googolplex refers to a very large number.

## REVISING   *Improving the Writing*

After reviewing her first draft, Hillary tried to make her writing clearer and more complete.  (The comments on the right side of her paper were made by a classmate.)

**Hillary changes the first line into a question.**

Who is

A Great Teacher ?

~~F~~unny, helpful, and friendly   What am I describing?  Is it one of ~~your~~ my classmates or ~~your~~ my best friend?  Beleive it or not, I'm describing ~~a~~ my math teacher!  His name is Mr. Vetter.  We call him Mr. V.

One thing that I really like about him is the way he makes learning fun.   *Why is this sentence all alone?*

If math seams boring, he will make it fun by

**She rewrites a wordy sentence.**

~~saying~~ something ~~that is so~~ funny so ~~you~~ we want to learn.  Once I sneezed really loud in the middle of class.  Right away, Mr. V. said "googolplex." It sounded just the same as gesundheit or bless you.

*Good example!*

Mr. V. also...

## EDITING & PROOFREADING

Hillary then made sure that her writing read smoothly and was free of errors. She paid special attention to spelling and punctuation. (She would check for errors one more time after writing a neat final draft of her paper.)

A Great Teacher

Who is funny, helpful, and friendly? Is it one

of my classmates or my best friend? Beleive it

or not, I'm describing my math teacher! His

*Hillary combines two sentences for smooth reading.*

name is Mr. Vetter, but we We call him Mr. V.

One thing that I really like about him is the

way he makes learning fun. If math seems seams

boring, he will say something funny so we want to

learn. Once I sneezed really loud in the middle of

*A comma and capital letter are added to the dialogue.*

class. Right away, Mr. V. said, "googolplex." It

sounded just the same as gesundheit or bless you.

Mr. V. also . . .

# A Basic Writing Guide

## Seven Secrets to Success

## 1 What should I write about?

Repeat this line after me: *I will write about a subject that really interests or excites me.* Say it again. Let this point be your guide each time you start a new writing project.

> **"** Writing has never been my best friend. I always thought it was hard, but now I'm able to pick better topics that I enjoy, and I have grown to love it. **"**
>
> —Shaun McDonnell, grade 5

See what I mean? Writing about something that interests you can make all the difference! It's what writing is all about.

**When you can't think of anything to write about, complete one of the selecting activities listed on pages 26-27.**

# 2 Do I have to collect a lot of details before I write?

That depends on the type of writing you are doing. If you're writing about a personal experience (like your first sleep-over), all of the important facts and details may be very clear to you. So you're probably ready to start your first draft right away.

But let's say you decide to write a classroom report about old-time movie monsters. You would have to collect quite a bit of information about this subject before you would be ready to write.

You can start your collecting by talking to someone about your subject or by writing down what you already know about it. Then you can go on from there by reading and trying other collecting activities.

**SEE** pages 30-31 for basic guidelines and activities to help you collect details for your writing.

# 3 Should I say everything I know about my subject?

No, your writing would probably go on and on if you say *everything* about it. So you have to think of some way to keep it under control. You can decide what your readers *really* need to know about your subject, and write just that information.

In addition, you can think of a focus, or main idea, for your writing. A focus may be a special feeling that you have about a subject, or it may be a certain part of a subject that you really want to talk about. For example, in a story about your best friend, you could focus on one of his or her important personality traits, like *kindness* or *loyalty*.

**SEE** page 32 for more information about planning your writing.

# 4  How should I write my first draft?

Write your first draft freely and honestly, as if you were telling it to a group of friends. Don't worry about making mistakes or using your best penmanship. In a first draft, you can cross out words, write in the margins, draw arrows, and so on. Remember that first drafts are often called *rough drafts*.

Also, don't worry about saying too much or too little about your subject. A first draft is only your first look at a writing idea; you will make changes later. If you have planning notes or a basic outline, use it as a guide when you write.

**SEE page 33 for more on writing first drafts.**

# 5  How do I know what changes to make in my first draft?

You are the best judge of your own writing. If important details seem to be missing, add them. If a certain part doesn't sound right, fix it. But it is also very important to have at least one or two classmates review your work. They may catch some important things that you didn't see.

When you revise, look first at the main points in your writing. Make sure that they are clear and complete. Once all of these ideas are in order, then look at more specific things like word choice and spelling.

**SEE pages 37-41 for more information about revising writing.**

# 6 Do I have to find all of the spelling and grammar errors in my writing?

Let's put it this way: No one expects you to be an expert speller or a master of all of the mechanics and grammar rules. But *everyone* expects you to correct as many errors as you can before you publish or share a piece of writing.  Writing that contains a lot of errors is hard to read.

Find as many errors as you can on your own. For example, you can make sure that each of your sentences begins with a capital letter and ends with a period.  Then ask a classmate or your teacher to check your work.  (All professional writers have editors who help them edit and proofread their work.)

**SEE pages 50-53 for more information on editing and proofreading.**

# 7 How do I know if my writing is good?

Here is a quick and simple way to evaluate your writing. If you can nod your head after at least three of these questions, you should feel good about your work.

_____ *Did you select a subject that really interests you?*

_____ *Did you think of a special way to write about this subject?*

_____ *Did you make changes in your writing until it said what you wanted it to say?*

_____ *Did you share your work during the writing process?*

**SEE page 45 for a basic checklist that will help you evaluate your writing.**

# Writing with a Computer

## Tools of the Trade

People simply can't work or play without the right tools. A family doctor couldn't carry out an examination without a stethoscope or tongue depressor (say ahhh!). A mechanic without socket wrenches and screwdrivers might as well close up shop. A spelunker, someone who explores caves, would be lost without a flashlight and hard hat.

Until you become quick on the keyboard, the personal computer will probably be most helpful to you as a revising and editing tool.

## All "Keyed Up"

One tool that many writers could not do without is the **personal computer**. Writers will tell you that a computer allows them to say a lot in a short amount of time. They will also tell you that revising and editing first drafts is very easy on the computer.

# Coming On-Line

Even if you don't have your own computer, your school is (or soon will be) equipped with them. If you are just learning to use a computer, the following comments about computers and writing will be helpful.

**Know Who's in Control** ➤ A computer can't think for you (not yet anyway), and it can't write for you. You still have to come up with all of the words and ideas.

**Know When to Use Your Computer** ➤ Don't put your pencils and paper away once you start using a computer (unless you are a keyboard wizard). You may want to do your planning and first drafts on paper. Then enter or type your work on the computer. At that point, you can make revising and editing changes on the computer screen or on a neat computer printout.

**Know What Your Computer Can Do** ➤ Word processing programs make a computer the high-tech writing machine it is. All programs allow you to enter your writing on the computer and work with it in many different ways. You can add or cut ideas and move parts around. You can check your work for spelling errors, and so on. (**SEE** the Bright Idea below.)

**Learn the Golden Rule** ➤ Expect to lose one of the first few assignments you write on a computer, even if you are very careful. It happens to everyone. Remember the golden rule of the computer age: *Always make a backup copy of your work.*

**Learn How to Keyboard** ➤ Practice keyboarding as often as you can—before, during, and after school. The faster you get, the more you will like using a computer. (**SEE** pages 422-423 for illustrations that will help you with this skill.)

To learn how your word processing program works, enter an old story or paragraph into the computer. Then practice making changes in your writing. (When you get stuck, refer to the program manual or ask a friend or classmate for help.)

# Planning Your Portfolio

## Organizing Your Own Writing

All writers keep a special collection of their work in a three-ring binder, in file folders, or in some other type of organizer. A collection like this is called a **personal portfolio**. My portfolio is in a three-ring binder, but I think of it more as a treasure chest— probably because all of the writing it contains is very special to me.

## One Writer's Portfolio

I've divided my portfolio into four sections: *new ideas, important drafts, writing just for me,* and *finished writing.* You can learn more about the different sections in my personal portfolio on the next page.

> 66 *Your portfolio represents your work as a writer. The pieces you include in it should say something about your personal talents and your writing process.* 99
> —Anne-Marie Oomen

## Personal Portfolio Model

Notice that my portfolio is basically organized according to the steps in the writing process.

---

**New Ideas** ● In this part of my portfolio, I collect interesting thoughts and descriptions scribbled on notebook paper, dinner napkins, and so on. I go to this section whenever I need ideas for writing.

**Important Drafts** ● This section includes writing projects that are almost finished. In one case, I may need to talk to someone about the writing. In another case, I may just need to get away from the writing for a while.

**Writing Just for Me** ● The writing in this section has great personal value to me, but I will never try to publish any of it. Included here are personal letters and special pages from my journal. Sometimes ideas for new writing projects come to mind as I reread this section.

**Finished Writing** ● I've taken all of these pieces through the entire writing process. They are as good as I can make them. Some of this work has already been published, and some of it I am still trying to get into print.

New Ideas

Important Drafts

Just for Me

Finished Writing

---

**Bright IDEA**

You might want to divide your personal portfolio according to the different types of writing you like to do: *poems, stories, plays,* and *letters.* Or you might want to divide it by different audiences: *personal and private, family, friends,* and so on. It's your choice.

# Preparing a Classroom Portfolio

If you do a lot of writing in your class, your teacher may ask you to put together a portfolio of your work at the end of the grading period. For a basic introduction to the classroom portfolio, read the next two pages.

## What is a classroom writing portfolio?

A classroom portfolio is a collection of the best writing you choose to turn in for evaluation. It will also contain basic self-evaluation sheets related to your writing, and maybe a few other things. (Your teacher will provide you with the self-evaluation sheets.)

## How is a classroom portfolio different from a basic writing folder?

A writing folder contains all of your in-class writing, from old assignments to the latest story you are working on. A portfolio, on the other hand, contains only your best efforts.

## Why would your teacher ask you to put together a portfolio?

Your teacher knows that a classroom portfolio makes the writing process much more real and meaningful for you. You are, after all, going to be judged on the writing *you* decide to include in your portfolio.

*❝I used to think of writing as my most dreaded fear. Now it's what I look forward to . . . When I look over my work, I feel honored that I wrote it. ❞*

—Kristen Tomlinson, grade 5

## What will you include?

Your teacher will make it very clear what your portfolio should contain. He or she will tell you how many pieces to include, what types of writing you can choose from, and when your portfolio must be ready.

## What is the most important thing to remember about a writing portfolio?

A writing portfolio is the story of your writing experiences. If you put forth your best efforts, your portfolio will be a success.

# Planning Tips

**Be Prepared** ● It's up to you to understand *all* of the requirements for your portfolio, including what it should contain and what it should look like. (Teachers usually provide special portfolio folders, but you might be able to design your own.)

**Stay Organized** ● Never, ever lose any of the drafts for writing you are going to include in your portfolio. (We will personally give you six lashes with a wet noodle for each draft you lose.)

**Keep on Schedule** ● Don't wait to the last minute to complete your writing or other parts of your portfolio. (Remember that it takes time to produce your best efforts.)

**Ask for Help** ● When you have questions about anything, ask your teacher and classmates for help. (Don't be bashful with something as important as a writing portfolio.)

**Do Your Best Work** ● All of your work should be neat and in the right place when you turn in your portfolio. (Try to make a good first impression.)

# Prewriting and Drafting Guide

**Building a File of Writing Ideas**

**Selecting a Subject**

**Starting Points for Writing**

**Collecting Details**

**Planning and Drafting Tips**

**Building a Resource of Writing Forms**

# Prewriting and Drafting Guide

**This section contains guidelines, lists, and suggestions for getting ready to write. We hope they help!**

Planning Tips

Writing Forms

Collecting Details

Writing Ideas

Starting Points

Selecting a Subject

BUILDING A FILE OF Writing IDEAS

Most writers are interesting people. They know a lot about all of the different things going on around them. And they try to remember and save as many details from their experiences as they can, knowing that these ideas can be used in their own writing. You can begin to save ideas, just like your favorite authors do, by completing some of the activities listed below. Have fun!

## Think and act like a writer!
Always keep your eyes and ears open for interesting sights and sounds. On the way to school, you might see two crazy squirrels dashing up and down a tree, as if they were running a shuttle race. In class, you might hear someone whisper, "What's the answer to number five?" Later at home, you might daydream about being famous someday. Without too much trouble, you could probably think of a story to write, using any one of these ideas.

**Helpful Hint** Reserve a section in a notebook or journal where you can list some of these sights and sounds.

## Keep track of your experiences!
Start a "This Is My Life" list and keep adding to it throughout the school year. Here's what you might include:

- People I'll Never Forget
- Animals I'll Never Forget
- Important Places Near and Far
- Favorite Books and Movies
- Special Skills and Talents
- Unforgettable Moments
- Biggest Blunders
- Important Beliefs
- Prized Possessions
- Wild Ideas

**_Make new discoveries!_**　Get involved in many different experiences. Join teams, visit different places, help people out, and have fun with friends. The more you do, the more you know.

**_Read a lot!_**　Read books, magazines, newspapers, and whatever else you like. Jot down any names, descriptions, or ideas that jump off the page as you read. These jottings may give you ideas for your own writing.

**_Write a lot!_**　Explore your thoughts and feelings in a personal journal or diary, and you will always have a good supply of writing ideas. (**_SEE_** pages 106-108 for more information.)

**_Draw a life map!_**　Start your life map with your birth and work right up to the present. Choose the experiences you want to picture along the way. This idea comes from two writers named Dan Kirby and Tom Liner. (See the model below.)

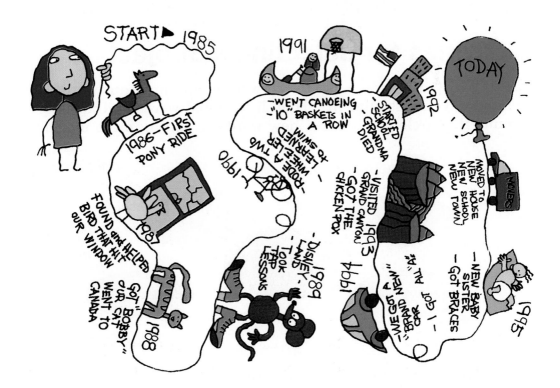

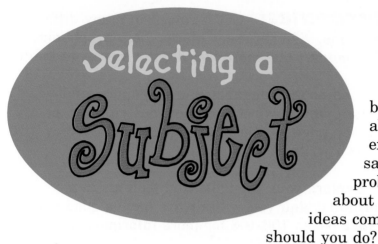

Let's say you've been asked to write about a memorable experience. You say to yourself, "No problem. I'll write about . . ." But then no ideas come to mind. What should you do?

First, see what your handbook has to say about your writing assignment. (Tips for selecting a subject are provided for many forms in "The Forms of Writing" section.) Then check your journal or writer's notebook for ideas. If you still need help, you can talk about the assignment with your classmates, or try one or more of the activities listed here.

# Activities for Selecting a Subject

**Clustering** ■ Begin a cluster by writing an important word related to your assignment. Then list related words and ideas around it. Circle and connect new words as shown in the model.

*Note:* After 2 or 3 minutes of clustering, a writing idea or two may begin to take shape. (Try free writing about one of these ideas.)

**Free Writing** ■ Write freely for 3 to 5 minutes. *Do not stop and think during this time; just write.* Begin free writing with an idea related to your assignment. As you write, one or two subjects may come to mind. (**SEE** pages 28-29 for ideas for free writing.)

**Listing** ■ Freely list any ideas that pop into your head when you think of your assignment. You and a classmate can help each other think of possible subjects by listing or brainstorming together.

**Sentence Completion** ■ Complete a sentence starter in as many ways as you can. Make sure that your sentence starter relates to your assignment. Here are six samples:

| | |
|---|---|
| I remember when . . . | I really get mad when . . . |
| One place I like . . . | I just learned . . . |
| I wonder how . . . | School is . . . |

**Review the Basics of Life Checklist** ■ Many of the things we need to lead a full life fall into the basic categories or groups listed below.

| | | |
|---|---|---|
| agriculture | faith | love |
| animals | family | machines |
| art/music | food | money |
| books | freedom | plants |
| clothing | friends | science/technology |
| community | health | work/play |
| education | housing | |
| energy | laws | |
| environment | | |
| exercise | | |

**MINI LESSON** Here's how you can use this checklist to think of possible subjects:

1. Choose one of the categories or groups. *(food)*
2. Decide how this category relates to your assignment. *(memorable experience)*
3. List possible subjects. *(your most memorable meal, a kitchen disaster, and so on)*

Starting **POINTS**
FOR WRITING

When you need a subject or starting point for a writing assignment, look at the prompts and topics on the next two pages for ideas.

# Writing Prompts

The following prompts will get you thinking about possible subjects for writing. For example, think of the many ways you could complete this phrase: "The first time I . . . ." You will find this page of prompts especially helpful when you are writing about a personal experience.

## Best and Worst

My best day
My worst moment
My biggest accomplishment
My saddest experience

## It could only happen to me!

It sounds unbelievable, but . . .
I felt so foolish.
I looked everywhere for . . .

## What if . . . and Why?

What if animals could talk?
What if I had three wishes?
Why is it important to win?
Why do we have to go so fast?

## Quotations

"Be yourself. Who else is better qualified?"
"Following the crowd can lead nowhere."
"Everyone needs a place to hang out."

## First and Last

The first time I . . .
My last visit with . . .
My first goal
The last place I want to go

## I Was Just Thinking

I believe in . . .
I worry about . . .
Things that make me angry

## School Days

I never worked so hard.
I'd like you to meet . . .
Where did I put my
    assignment!

"More is not always better."
"We all make mistakes."
"Take life one day at a time."

# Writing Topics

As you can see, the following topics are organized according to the four basic reasons for writing.  They will be especially helpful when you need ideas for a specific kind of writing (descriptions, explanations, narratives, and persuasive paragraphs).

## Describing

**People:** a relative, a teacher, a classmate, a neighbor, someone who bugs you, someone you spend time with, someone you wish you were like

**Places:** your room, a garage, a basement, an attic, a rooftop, the alley, the gym, the library, a barn, a lake, a river, a yard, a park, the zoo, a museum

**Objects or things:** a poster, a stuffed animal, a video game, a book, a drawing, a junk drawer, a photograph, a letter, a pet, a souvenir, a model, a key, a dream

## Explaining

**How to . . .** make a taco, care for a pet, impress a teacher, earn extra money, get in shape, be a friend, stop hiccups, run a race, saddle a horse, teach . . . , choose . . . , build . . . , fix . . . , grow . . . , save . . . , find . . .

**The causes of . . .** rust, acid rain, friendship, hurricanes, happiness

**Kinds of . . .** music, commercials, clouds, heroes, cars, pain, groups, restaurants, fun, streets, stores, books

**The definition of . . .** love, learning, a good time, friendship, a team, equality, a teacher, courage

## Persuading

school rules, homework, smoking in public places, shoplifting, carrying guns, air bags, something that needs improving, something that's unfair, something everyone should see or do, something worth supporting

## Narrating (Sharing)

getting caught, getting lost, getting together, making a mistake, being surprised, making the news, learning to _____ , being scared, winning

**TAKE NOTE** Try writing freely about one of the prompts or topics related to your assignment.  As you write, you may discover a number of possible writing ideas.

You really have three basic ways to collect facts and details about a subject.  You can . . .

✔ talk to someone about it,

✔ read and learn about it yourself,

✔ and try one or more of the following collecting activities.

**Free Writing** ■ Let's say your subject for a writing assignment is the first time you slept over at a friend's house.  If you write freely about this time, you will see how many details you really remember about it. *Don't stop and think for this type of writing; just keep the ideas flowing.*  (Sometimes your free writing will be so good that you can use it as your first draft.)

To give your free writing a special twist, write to a specific audience: a group of preschoolers, your parents, a student from another country, etc.

**5 W's of Writing** ■ Answer the 5 W's—*Who? What? When? Where?* and *Why?*—to collect basic information about your subject. (Add *How?* to the list for even more details.)

**Clustering** ■ Use the subject of your writing as the nucleus word for a cluster.  Then list, circle, and connect words related to your subject.  (***SEE*** page 26 for a model.)

**Subject Talk** ■ Make up a dialogue in which two people (real or imaginary) talk about your subject.  Keep the conversation going as long as you can.

## Focused Thinking ■ To think carefully about a subject, write freely about it in two or three of the following ways:

☐ *Describe it.* What do you see, hear, feel, smell, taste?

☐ *Compare it.* What is it like? What is it different from?

☐ *Apply it.* What can you do with it? How can you use it?

☐ *Break it down.* What parts does it have? How do they work?

☐ *Evaluate it.* What are its strengths and weaknesses?

## Crazy Questions ■ To help you see your subject in creative ways, make up some crazy questions about it, and then try to answer them. Some sample questions follow:

### Writing About a Person
*What type of clothing is this person like?*
*Which city or place should this person never visit?*

### Writing About a Place
*What does this place like to do?*
*What song does it like?*

### Writing About an Object
*What does this object do on weekends?*
*What does it look like upside down?*

### Writing to Explain a Process
*Where does this process like to shop?*
*What sport is it like?*

### Writing About an Experience (a Narrative)
*What movie is this experience like?*
*What colors does it call to mind?*

## Collection Sheet ■ Use a collection sheet or gathering grid to help you keep track of the facts and details you collect. (**SEE** pages 173 and 226 for examples.)

PLANNING AND Drafting Tips

All successful sports teams start out with a game plan. This plan keeps them organized and focused as the game starts. A game plan (a writing plan) can help you do the same thing when you start a first draft. Here's one way you might draw up your plan.

# Developing a Writing Plan

**The First Step** ➤ Start with these five important points:

> **Subject:** *Who or what are you writing about?*
>
> **Purpose:** *Why are you writing? (To explain? To describe?)*
>
> **Form/Organization:** *What form will you use (poem, paragraph, etc.)?*
>
> **Audience:** *Who are your readers?*
>
> **Voice:** *How will your writing sound (serious, funny, etc.)?*

**A Sample Plan** ➤ Let's say I plotted out the following assignment:

> **Subject:** My best friend, Roy
>
> **Purpose:** To describe why I like him
>
> **Form/Organization:** Letter
>
> **Audience:** Classmates and Roy
>
> **Voice:** Friendly

**The Next Step** ➤ Next, I would decide on the type of ideas I want to include. I could, for example, write about the funny things Roy does, or the different things we like to do together.

At this point, I would be well prepared to write. I would know who I was writing about, how I wanted my writing to look, and what I wanted to say. (If something in my plan didn't work out, I could always change part of it.)

# Writing a First Draft

Remember that your first draft is your first look at your writing, so it doesn't have to be (and shouldn't be) perfect. Don't stop and think and worry. Just write freely. All you need to do is get your main ideas on paper.

**Be Prepared** ● It is always easier to write a first draft when you know a lot of facts and details about your subject, and you have a basic plan to follow.

**Be Willing to Work** ● Write your draft while all of your collecting and planning are still fresh in your mind.

**Be Open-minded** ● If some new ideas pop into your mind as you write, don't be afraid to include them in your writing.

**Be Honest** ● Let the real you come through in your writing. This is your paper, so make it sound like you!

You may want to talk about your ideas with a classmate or friend before you actually begin to write. Sharing your thoughts can help you test them out before you write them down. Talking can also help you write more freely and naturally.

## Plan the Opening Sentences

Sometimes it helps to plan exactly what you want to say in the opening sentences before you dive into your first draft. Make sure your first lines sound interesting. But also make sure that they state your true feelings about your subject.

You may want to start your writing in one of the following ways:

■ Begin with a surprising fact or quote.

■ Start with a question.

■ Open with some dialogue.

■ Share a brief story about the subject.

■ Introduce some of the main points you plan to cover.

Helpful **SEE** "Writing a Lead" on page 130 for more ideas and
Hint    examples.

BUILDING A
RESOURCE OF
Writing
Forms

Have you ever written and designed a storybook? Have you ever created your own bumper sticker or written your own book of riddles? Just thinking about all of the forms of writing available to you might help you to write.

Advertisements
Autobiographies
Biographies
Book Reviews
Bumper Stickers
Cartoons, Comic Strips
Descriptions
Dialogues
Dictionaries
Directions (how-to)
Editorials
Family Parables
Instructional Manuals
Interviews
Jokes
Journals, Diaries
Letters

Myths
Narratives
Newspaper Writing
Pamphlets
Photo Captions
Plays
Poems
Proposals
Radio Plays
Recipes
Reports
Requests
Reviews
Riddles
Slogans
Songs
Tall Tales
Time Lines

## *Other Forms You Might Try*

**Anecdote** ● a little story used to make a point

**Aphorism** ● a short, wise saying

**Bio-poem** ● a poem about someone's life

**Case Study** ● a story of one person who represents a larger group

**Character Sketch** ● a description of a real person

**Commentary** ● a personal opinion about the state of the world

**Dramatic Monologue** ● a one-way conversation in which someone tells a lot about him- or herself

**E-mail** (electronic mail) ● a message sent between two people using computers

**News Release** ● an explanation of a coming event using the 5 W's

**Observation Report** ● writing that records sights, sounds, and other sensory details

**Oral History** ● writing down tape-recorded or filmed conversation about an earlier time period

**Parody** ● a funny imitation of a serious piece of writing

**Pet Peeve** ● a personal feeling about something that bugs you

**Petition** ● a formal request addressed to someone in power

**Profile** ● a detailed report about a person

**Time Capsule** ● writing that captures a particular time period

**Travelogue** ● writing that describes travel pictures (slides, video, film)

**THINK IT OVER**

You can learn a lot about writing by experimenting with many of these forms. For example, by writing photo captions, you may learn something that will help you write more effective descriptive paragraphs.

# Revising and Editing Guide

**Revising Your Writing**

**Conferencing with Partners**

**Sharing Family Stories**

**Editing and Proofreading**

**Publishing Your Writing**

# Revising Checklist

Use the following checklist as a guide when you review and revise a first draft.

____ *Did I focus on a certain part of my subject, instead of trying to say everything about it?*

____ *Do I need to add any information?*
- ✔ Do I need to add a topic sentence, or a sentence that states the main idea of my writing?
- ✔ Do I need to add any important details?
- ✔ Do I need to add a closing or concluding sentence?

____ *Do I need to cut any information?*
- ✔ Did I include any details that don't support my main idea?
- ✔ Have I repeated myself in any parts?
- ✔ Have I said too much about a certain idea?

____ *Do I need to rewrite any parts?*
- ✔ Are there ideas or sentences that are unclear or confusing?
- ✔ Did I do too much telling and not enough showing? (**SEE** the next page.)
- ✔ Could I improve my explanation in a certain part?

____ *Do I need to reorder any parts of my writing?*
- ✔ Do any ideas or details seem to be out of place?
- ✔ Did I place my most important point in the best spot?
- ✔ Did I follow an effective method of organization? (**SEE** page 68.)

# Show Don't Tell

If you do a lot of telling in your first draft, try turning it into writing that shows. If readers can't *see* and *hear* and *touch* and *taste* and *feel* what you've written, it just won't come to life for them. Here's the basic rule:

**Use your five senses as you write, and show your readers what you mean.**

## One Writer in Action

Here's how author Will Hobbs explains writing that shows.

*Let's say I almost drowned last summer, and I'm trying to tell a reader what it was like: "I was drowning. It was really bad. I thought I was going to die. I was really scared . . ." Now, does the reader feel what it was like? The answer is no. Did I tell, or did I show? I told. I didn't use the five senses.*

**Don't Use "Telling" Words ▪** I try not to use words that tell, like "scared" or "angry." When Cloyd is walking out on a high ledge in my novel *Bearstone*, I didn't want to tell the readers he was scared. I tried to show them instead.

**Use "Showing" Words ▪** *"The shape of the rock had forced his body weight out over the thin air, and he was in bad trouble. Stretched tight, the tendons above his heels began to quiver, then to tremble. His strength deserted him in a rush. He paused to rest, but his legs began to shake violently."*

# More Revising Tips

## Check for Details

*"I went to my first basketball game. It was fun."*

These two sentences don't say much, do they? We don't know who went to the game, who played, who won, and so on. In other words, a lot of details are missing. Always make sure that you have included enough details in your writing.

## Include a Beginning, Middle, and Ending

Your writing should be clear and complete from start to finish. That means it should contain an effective beginning, middle, and ending.

**Beginning:** Make sure your opening lines grab your readers' attention and tell them something about your subject:

*"Listen everybody. Let's keep our buses clean!"*

**Middle:** Stick to the point! All of the ideas in the middle, or body, of your writing should support or explain your subject.

**Ending:** Add a closing idea to stress the importance of your subject and to keep your reader thinking about it:

*"I've seen enough ABC gum, paper wads, and old Kleenex to last me a long time. I hope you have, too."*

## Add a Title

Once you have all of your main ideas in place, think of a title for your writing. List a number of possible choices, and select the best one. A good title should hook your readers into your writing:

*Four Quarters of Fun* sounds better than *My First Game.*

*Have Garbage Will Travel* sounds better than *Bus Litter.*

You may have to revise your writing two or three times before all of your ideas are clear and complete.

# Conferencing with Partners

## Sharing and Learning

Writers spend a lot of time thinking and writing by themselves. But sooner or later they need an audience, someone to listen to what they've written. Do you ever nudge your neighbor at school and say, "Hey, Josh, listen to this"? Or at home, do you ever ask your mom or dad to react to something you are writing? If you do, you are acting like a real author.

## Getting Started

This chapter is all about working in writing groups and helping one another become better listeners, thinkers, and writers.

Anytime writers share ideas about their writing, they are having a conference. You can conference in pairs or in small groups, in school or at home, with classmates or with your teacher, with friends or with family members.

# Counting on Your Friends

All good writers (like you!) know they need to find someone who will listen to their writing and help them make it better. Fifth graders in room 18 at Wixom Elementary in Wixom, Michigan, gave these reasons for talking with their classmates in writing conferences:

## Conference partners help writers . . .

- think about all of the ideas in their writing,
- discover new ideas to add to their writing,
- and learn new skills (like writing dialogue).

## A good conference partner . . .

- makes you feel comfortable,
- helps you stay on track (so you don't talk too much about recess),
- shows an interest in your subject,
- listens carefully,
- and gives you straight answers.

*“When I conferenced, I became friends with more people. I felt wonderful because I knew some of me was in their writing. ”*
—Damian Broccoli, grade 5

# Helping One Another

Conference partners can help you throughout the writing process. Their advice is especially important once you complete a first draft. They can help you identify the parts that work well in your writing, as well as the parts that need work.

They can also help you when you are ready to edit and proofread your work. Good conference partners will catch the spelling or grammar errors that you miss. Finally, they can react to the final draft of your writing. This is the most exciting (and perhaps the scariest) part of the writing process.

# Conference Guidelines

During a conference, authors read their drafts to partners who listen and respond. Listed below are tips for conference partners.

## Suggestions for Authors:

- Come prepared with a piece of writing you really care about.
- Tell your partner about your interest in this writing.
- Point out any problems you're having.
- Read your work out loud. (Speak clearly and don't rush.)
- Pay attention to what your partner tells you is working or not working in your draft. (His or her questions and suggestions will help you improve your writing.)
- Don't take suggestions personally. Your partner is just trying to help.

## Suggestions for Listeners:

- Listen carefully (and take notes) so you can make good observations. (**SEE** "Good Listener Checklist," page 293.)
- Begin your response with positive comments. ("I like the way . . .")
- Ask questions if you are confused about something or want to know more. ("What do you mean when you say . . .?")
- Make suggestions in a helpful way. (Don't say, "Your writing is boring." Try something like, "Many of your sentences begin in the same way.")
- And always be kind and polite. Writers work hard!

**THINK IT OVER**

Conference partners should praise a classmate when they like something in his or her writing, but they should really mean it. Writing conferences should not be popularity contests.

# Response Sheets

How can you help an author remember all of your comments and suggestions?  You can write them down on a response sheet.  Your teacher may already have response sheets for you to complete.  If not, it is easy enough to make up your own.  Here are two ideas.

### Memorable

On the top half of a sheet of paper, write the word "Memorable."  List the things you really like about a piece of writing under this word.

### More

Halfway down this sheet, write the word "More."  List one or two suggestions or questions you may have under this word.

## Checklist

**Organization:**

✔ Does the writing have a beginning, a middle, and an end?
✔ Are all of the ideas arranged in the best order?

**Details:**

✔ Do all of the details support the subject (topic sentence)?
✔ Are enough details and examples included?

**Style:**

✔ Is the writing easy to follow?
✔ Does the writing contain interesting or descriptive words and ideas?

**Mechanics:**

✔ Is the writing accurate (free of careless spelling and punctuation errors)?
✔ Is the writing neatly presented?

# Sharing Family Stories

## Tell Me Again

Sharing stories can be a very powerful learning tool. Each time you listen to one of your classmate's stories, and tell him or her what interests you about it, you are helping your classmate and yourself grow as writers. Writing and sharing go hand in hand. **We write to share; we share to write better.**

## Writing and Learning

As you learn how to write family stories in this chapter, you will also be provided with guidelines for sharing your work. (You will also use some of the conferencing tips included in the last chapter.) The experience you gain here will make it that much easier for you to share your work in the future.

You can also expect to have a lot of fun. Sharing family stories is a very enjoyable thing to do.

> **❝ Everybody has heard family stories . . . The fun of hearing about my grandfather's life taught me to listen with pleasure. ❞**
> — Marie Ponsot

# Finding Family Parables

In all my years of school, I've never studied a subject called "My Grandpa." But I know him better than the multiplication table. I've visited him at work. I've watched him at his hobby, making fine things out of wood. I especially remember the maple boxes and building blocks he used to make. And best of all, I've heard him talk.

What happened around us usually reminded Grandpa of something, and then he'd tell us a story about it. I loved that. Today I call these stories **family parables.**

## The Older, the Better

Everybody has heard family parables. Older folks often tell really good ones—the ones that have been told most often, for the longest time. Just think, many grandparents were alive 50 years ago. When they talk about *their* grandparents, they are telling stories that might be 100 years old. But don't forget your parents and aunts and uncles; they, too, have a lot of good family stories to share.

## Student Model

Student writer Charles Vodak will never forget the following family story. It has been told to him time and time again. (As you can see, some family stories can be very short.)

My mom always tells me this story when we're at my grandmother's house.

When my mom was a little girl, she had to share a room with my Aunt Ann. My mom's side of the room was clean, but my aunt's side was always a mess. One day my aunt cleaned her closet, and she found some kittens in there. And guess what? They didn't even have a cat!

# Writing a Family Story

Lots of family parables are about times of change or about trying something new. Such stories sleep in our memories till a word or an experience calls them to mind. They haunt a happy part of our thoughts. It's a part we can't always get at directly. But stories will come to us, once we search them out.

## PREWRITING *Planning Your Writing*

**Select a Subject** ● Begin your subject search by telling a brief family story to a friend or classmate. Listen to one of hers or his. Tell another. Listen again. As you do, you'll get a feel for one or two stories that you might like to write about.

Helpful Hint   If you are working by yourself, complete this sentence starter: "I remember the story of . . ." Then continue listing ideas until you hit upon a subject.

## WRITING THE FIRST DRAFT

**Start Writing** ● Once you select a favorite family parable, the next step is to write it down from memory. I like to begin my writing with a one-sentence introduction. For instance, I'll write, "This is a story my grandmother told during a thunderstorm." Then I start the actual story in a new paragraph.

**Keep It Going** ● There are no rules about how long or how short a family parable should be. That will depend on how it was told to you, and how you remember it.

*Now, stop reading, choose a favorite story from your list, and begin to write your parable.*

## REVISING    *Improving Your Writing*

**Share Your Writing** ● Read your first draft aloud to a small group of classmates. Make sure to read loudly enough and slowly enough for everyone to hear your words.

After the reading, members of your group should take turns telling you what they liked about your parable. Listen carefully, so you can do more of these things the next time you write.

Now listen to other members of your group read their stories. Share your ideas about each story. (The more often you respond to someone's writing, the better writer you will become.)

**Review Your First Draft** ● After the sharing session is over, review your first draft on your own. Then consider any changes you would like to make in your work.

## EDITING & PROOFREADING

**Edit Carefully** ● Make sure your parable reads smoothly and clearly from start to finish. Also check for spelling, punctuation, and grammar errors. A family story should be treated with a great deal of respect, so edit it carefully.

**Proofread Your Final Draft** ● Type or write a neat final copy of your work. Then check it one last time for any periods or capital letters you may have missed.

MINI LESSON    You should also practice making written observations about shared stories. Follow these steps:

❑ Ask one author to read his or her story aloud.

❑ Write about what you remember. An easy way to practice this kind of writing is to begin with "It interests me that . . ." and then add whatever you like to complete the sentence. List as many "interests" as you can.

❑ Share your written observations about this story as a group.

❑ Take turns listening, observing, and responding to the stories.

# Editing and Proofreading

## Polishing Your Writing

This chapter deals with editing and proofreading, the step in the writing process when you get your writing ready to share or publish. Remember that editing and proofreading becomes important *after* you have changed, or revised, any of the main ideas in your first draft.

## Make Every Word Count!

The guidelines in this chapter will help you check your writing for style and correctness. All of your sentences and words should read smoothly, and they should be free of careless errors. In other words, this chapter will help you make every word count in your work.

**❝ I think about what I write, and put great care into picking the words I use. ❞**
—Catherine Ferrante, student

# Checking Your Sentences

**Combine Short Sentences** ● If you use too many short sentences one after another, your writing may sound choppy. You can correct this problem by combining some of your sentences.

Four short sentences:

> *The dog followed Mary.*
> *It followed her for half a mile.*
> *It stayed very close behind her.*
> *She forced herself to stay calm.*

■ **Two Longer, Smoother Sentences:**

> *The dog followed Mary for half a mile. It stayed very close behind her, but she forced herself to stay calm.*

**Change Your Sentence Beginnings** ● If too many of your sentences begin in the same way, your writing may sound dull and lifeless. You can correct this problem by changing the way you start some of your sentences.

Three sentences beginning with the subject *I*:

> *I slowly ate the cooked carrots. I washed them down with milk to cover the taste. I tried to hide some of them when my mom wasn't looking.*

## How to Change Sentence Beginnings

■ **Start with a Modifier:**

> *Slowly, I ate the cooked carrots.*

■ **Start with a Phrase:**

> *To cover the taste, I washed them down with milk.*

■ **Start with a Clause:**

> *When my mom wasn't looking, I tried to hide some of them.*

**Correct Sentence Errors** ● There are three basic types of errors you should look for in your writing: *sentence fragments, run-on sentences,* and *rambling sentences.* (**SEE** page 87.)

# Checking for Word Choice

**Use Powerful Verbs** ● As writer Will Hobbs says, "Verbs power sentences, making them fly or jump or sink or swim." They help make your ideas come alive for your readers. Here are two sentences from *Bearstone* by Will Hobbs. The powerful verbs (in bold type) give an effective picture of the action.

> The big fish **flip-flopped** against Cloyd's leg. He **nudged** it back into the water with his foot, then **leaped** across the Rincon stream.

**Use Specific Nouns** ● Some nouns like *car, fruit, store, flowers,* and *candy* are general and give readers a fuzzy picture. Other nouns like **Dodge Shadow**, **kiwi, K-Mart**, **tulips**, and **Snickers** are specific and give readers a much clearer picture. Always try to use specific nouns in your writing.

**Choose Colorful Modifiers** ● Effective adjectives and adverbs can add color to your writing.

- ■ **Using Adjectives:**

  *She wandered into the **deep** shade of the **giant** cottonwoods.* (The adjectives make the picture clearer.)

- ■ **Using Adverbs:**

  *Rover ran **wildly** after Rachael. She headed **directly** for the back door.* (The adverbs add to the action.)

 Modifiers are very important to use, but be careful not to *overuse* them. Too many adjectives and adverbs can make your writing sound unnatural.

**Select the Right Word** ● Make sure that the words you use in your writing are correct. For example, it's easy to confuse words that sound the same—*there, their,* and *they're; know* and *no.* (**SEE** pages 362-369 for a list of words that are often confused.)

# Editing and Proofreading Checklist

Use this checklist as a guide when you edit your writing. Also use it when you are ready to proofread your final draft.

## Sentence Structure

✔ Did I write clear and complete sentences?

✔ Did I write sentences of different lengths?

✔ Did I begin my sentences in different ways?

## Punctuation

✔ Does each sentence end with an end punctuation mark?

✔ Did I use commas in a series (*Larry, Moe, and Curly*)?

✔ Did I place commas before connecting words (*and, but, or*) in compound sentences?

✔ Did I punctuate dialogue correctly?  (**SEE** pages 346 and 350 for help.)

## Capitalization

✔ Did I start all my sentences with a capital letter?

✔ Did I capitalize nouns that name specific people, places, and things?

## Usage

✔ Did I use powerful verbs, specific nouns, and colorful modifiers?

✔ Did I use the correct word (*to, too,* or *two; your* or *you're*)?  (**SEE** pages 362-369 for help.)

## Spelling

✔ Did I check for spelling?  Did I use the spell checker on my computer?  (**SEE** pages 270-273 for help.)

# Publishing Your Writing

## The Final Step

Publishing is a very important part of the writing process. It makes all of your planning, drafting, and revising worth the effort. And it also gets other people to listen to your ideas.

Publishing can take many forms. Reading a finished story to your classmates is a form of publishing—so is selecting a poem for your classroom portfolio. If your classmates and teacher really like your writing, you might want to explore some of the following ways to publish it.

## *Mail It!*

Greeting cards

**Letters to public figures**

Requests for information

*Thank-you letters to field-trip guides, bus drivers, etc.*

Letters that complain about or praise a product or service

**Letters to pen pals in other schools, cultures, or countries**

*Notes to parents about school activities*

## Perform It!

Plays for school and community audiences
  **Puppet shows**
Radio shows over the school public address system
  **Talking books for the visually impaired**
Taped interviews for a class project
  **New words for familiar music**
Presentations at PTA or school board meetings
  **Introductions of guests at assemblies**
Videotaped documentaries for local TV stations

## Print It!

- All-school or classroom collections
- *Stories just for veterinarian clinics, doctors' offices, or other waiting rooms*
- Manuals on how to do certain things
- *School-survival guides for younger students*
- Programs for school productions
- *Newspaper reports of class trips or projects*
- School handbook updates
- *Kid's-eye-view brochures for local travel agency or chamber of commerce*

# Submit It!

There are many magazines published every month that feature student writing. Write to one that you think might publish your work. Ask your teacher for help. Also ask your teacher or librarian for a list of contests you can send your writing to.

## Magazines That Publish Student Work

### Owl

**Topics:** Environment/Science/Nature

**Forms:** Letters, drawings, poetry, short short stories

**Address:** *Owl*, Editor
179 John St., Suite 500
Toronto, Ontario
CANADA M5T 3G5

### Skipping Stones

**Topics:** Multicultural/Nature

**Forms:** Fiction, songs, games, true stories, poems, essays

**Address:** *Skipping Stones*, Editor
P.O. Box 3939
Eugene, OR 97403

### Highlights for Children

**Topics:** General

**Forms:** Fiction, poems, true stories, letters to the editor

**Address:** Children's Mail
803 Church Street
Honesdale, PA 18431

### Daybreak Star

**Topics:** Native American Life

**Forms:** Essays, fiction, poems, true stories

**Address:** Unified Indians of All
Tribes Foundation
1945 Yale Place East
Seattle, WA 98102

### Creative Kids

**Topics:** Writing

**Forms:** Book reviews, essays, fiction, crafts/hobbies, riddles, poems, true stories

**Address:** Prufrock Press,
Submission Editor
P.O. Box 8813
Waco, TX 76714

### Stone Soup

**Topics:** Writing/Art

**Forms:** Stories, poems

**Address:** *Stone Soup*, Editor
P.O. Box 83
Santa Cruz, CA 95063

(You must include a self-addressed stamped envelope.)

*❝ It feels wonderful to be an author of a real story. I like to publish my writing because it is like making my ideas come alive! ❞*

—Stephen Greenberg, grade 5

## *Bind It!*

To make or bind your own book for publication, follow these six basic steps. Make sure to add your own personal touches as you put your book together.

**1** Stack in order the pages to be bound and add extra pages for titles, etc.

**2** Staple or sew the pages together.

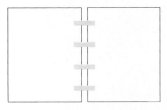

**3** Cut two pieces of cardboard 1/4 inch larger than the page size. Tape them together.

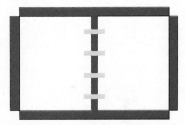

**4** Place the cardboard on the cover material (contact paper or glue-on wallpaper). Turn the edges of the cover material over the cardboard.

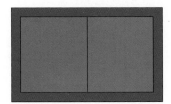

**5** Attach construction paper or contact paper to the inside of the book cover.

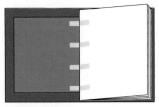

**6** Fasten the bound pages of the book into the cover with tape.

# Building Paragraphs and Essays

Writing Paragraphs

Writing Essays

A Writing Sampler

# Writing Paragraphs

## What Is a Paragraph?

A paragraph is a group of sentences that tells about one subject or idea. Each sentence in a paragraph must give information about the topic. And the sentences must be in the right order, so your readers can understand the information.

A good paragraph presents a complete and interesting picture. The specific subject is stated in one sentence—usually the topic sentence. All of the facts and details in the rest of the sentences add to the readers' understanding of the subject. In other words, all of the parts work together.

In this chapter, paragraphs are explained, the different parts are named, and the basic types are identified. Step-by-step tips for writing good paragraphs are also given.

# The Basic Parts of a Paragraph

You can think of a paragraph as a train. The **topic sentence** is the train's engine. It's the main idea that all the other sentences are connected to. The sentences in the **body** of the paragraph are the boxcars. They carry the paragraph's "cargo"—facts, figures, examples. The **closing sentence** is the caboose. It doesn't carry cargo; it just sums up what went before.

**The Topic Sentence** ● A paragraph begins with a *topic sentence*: a sentence that tells the reader what the paragraph is about. A topic sentence has two main parts—a specific subject and a focus.

**The subject:** The **subject** of a topic sentence has to be specific or small enough to explain in one paragraph. You couldn't write a paragraph on "the history of baseball." It would be too long! But you could write a paragraph on "yesterday's softball game." That subject is more specific!

**The focus:** You need more than a subject to write a topic sentence. You also need a **focus**. A focus is usually a feeling or an attitude about the subject. It lets the reader know what you're going to say about the subject.

MINI LESSON   Here is a simple **formula** that makes it easy to write good topic sentences. Use it whenever you have to write a paragraph.

> **Subject** (Who? or What?)
> + **Feeling/Focus** (What about it?)
> ―――――――――――――――――――
> = **Topic Sentence**

## Sample Topic Sentence

> *In yesterday's softball game* (specific subject), *the fourth grade pounded the fifth grade* (focus).

**The Body** ● The middle of the paragraph is called the *body*. It includes the sentences between the topic sentence and the closing sentence. These sentences must give the reader all the information needed to understand the topic. Below are sentences that could follow the topic sentence in a paragraph about "yesterday's softball game."

## Sample Body

*When the fourth grade batted, Tim started off with a double. Jamie batted next and hit a home run. The fifth grade scored two runs in the third inning to tie the score. After Sarah hit a grand slam for the fourth grade in the next inning, the fifth grade never scored again.*

**The Closing Sentence** ● A paragraph ends with a *closing sentence*. This sentence may sum up the information in the paragraph, or tell what it means. Below is a sample closing sentence that could be used after the "Sample Body" above.

## Sample Closing Sentence

*Thanks to Sarah's grand slam, the fourth grade won by four runs.*

 If you put the *Sample Topic Sentence, Sample Body,* and *Sample Closing Sentence* together, you'll have a **Sample Paragraph!**

In yesterday's softball game, the fourth grade pounded the fifth grade. When the fourth grade batted, Tim started off with a double. Jamie batted next and hit a home run. The fifth grade scored two runs in the third inning to tie the score. After Sarah hit a grand slam for the fourth grade in the next inning, the fifth grade never scored again. Thanks to Sarah's grand slam, the fourth grade won by four runs.

# Types of Paragraphs

There are four kinds of paragraphs you can write.

- ■ To describe something, write a **descriptive** paragraph.
- ■ To tell a story, write a **narrative** paragraph.
- ■ To express your opinion, write a **persuasive** paragraph.
- ■ To explain something, write an **expository** paragraph.

## Descriptive Paragraph

A **descriptive** paragraph describes a person, a place, a thing, or an idea. When you write a descriptive paragraph, you should use words that help your readers see, hear, smell, taste, and feel what you are describing. You should tell your readers what colors things are, how big things are, what things sound like, etc. Your readers should feel as if they are right there with you.

### Model Descriptive Paragraph

You can tell a lot about Evan by looking at his face. The first thing you notice are his big brown eyes that always seem so shiny and alert. You wouldn't notice his pug nose except that it seems to be running all of the time. Like many little boys, he wipes it with his sleeve rather than a Kleenex. His mouth seems to have two basic positions. He smiles when he's got trouble on his mind, or he clenches his mouth shut when he doesn't want to do something, like eat his lunch. Evan's tongue, which he likes to stick out, is usually orange from his favorite fruit drink. Whenever someone tries to clean his mouth or chin, he squirms and turns away. Evan likes his face just the way it is.

# Narrative Paragraph

In a **narrative** paragraph, you tell a story by sharing the details of an experience.  A narrative paragraph should pull your readers into the story and keep them wondering what will happen next.  It's important to include a lot of colorful details to make the experience come alive.

## Model Narrative Paragraph

Evan leaves a trail of trouble even when he isn't trying. The last time I baby-sat for him, we were painting pictures at the kitchen table. Evan painted a couple of monster faces, and then decided he wanted to do something else. He even offered to help clean up, which surprised me a little. He was carrying the bowl full of dirty water from our paint brushes when disaster struck. He tripped right in front of the sink in the utility room and the dirty water went flying. I did my best to clean up the mess while Evan had a snack. As I worked, I reminded myself never to let Evan help again.

**Bright IDEA**

To make sure you have included all the important details in your narrative paragraph, ask the following questions: *Who? What? When? Where? Why? How?*

## Persuasive Paragraph

A **persuasive** paragraph gives the writer's opinion on the topic and tries to get the reader to agree with it. When you write a persuasive paragraph, you should give facts and examples to back up your opinion. Otherwise, you won't *persuade,* or convince, your reader that your opinion is the right one.

## Model Persuasive Paragraph

Anyone who baby-sits for Evan should receive an extra bonus. For one thing, you have to put up with Evan's screaming. He likes to sneak up behind you and scream in your ear. He's very good at scaring just about anyone with this move. For another thing, you never get a chance to rest for even a minute. Evan likes to keep things active by teasing the cat, locking himself in his room, overloading the circuits, falling off his bike, and so on. And finally, you have to clean up after him. There is always spilled milk to wipe up in the kitchen and dumped toys to pick up in every other room. For conditions like these, the regular hourly rate is not enough!

Helpful Hint  Read your paragraph out loud so that you can listen for missing information. Also turn to page 309 in your handbook for more on using facts and opinions in your writing.

# Expository Paragraph

The main purpose of an **expository** paragraph is to give information about a topic. It may explain ideas, give directions, or show how to do something. An expository paragraph uses transition words (such as *first, second,* and *most importantly* in the model below). These words help guide the reader through the explanation.

## Model Expository Paragraph

Always be prepared when you baby-sit for Evan. First, make sure to bring a flashlight in case of a blackout. Evan likes to overload the circuits. Second, bring a few first-aid supplies like cotton balls and Band-Aids. Evan will get at least two or three scratches or cuts while you are there, and sometimes their first-aid kit is low on materials. You can also use the cotton balls to plug your ears if Evan starts screaming. Most importantly, have a phone number where you can contact Evan's mother. No matter how prepared you are, you can't baby-sit for Evan all by yourself. You will need to call his mother at least once for help or advice.

**TAKE NOTE**

Sometimes it's helpful to list the facts or examples you are going to include in your paragraph. That way, you can put your supporting ideas into the best possible order before you begin.

## Sample Listing

**Topic Sentence:** *Always be prepared when you baby-sit for Evan.*
- ✔ *Bring a flashlight*
- ✔ *Bring first-aid supplies*
- ✔ *Have a phone number to contact his mother*

# Writing the Paragraph

**1** **Plan your paragraph.** To begin planning your paragraph, you can ask yourself the following questions:

**Subject:** *Who or what will I write about?*

**Purpose:** *What feeling about my subject will I focus on?*

**Audience:** *Who will be reading my paragraph?*

**Form:** *What kind of paragraph will work best?*

**2** **Gather information.** Once you've answered these questions, you are ready to begin gathering details for your paragraph. This chart will help you decide what information you need to collect.

| *For a . . .* | *you'll need . . .* |
|---|---|
| **descriptive paragraph** | lots of details about how things look, sound, smell, feel, etc. |
| **narrative paragraph** | details about an experience you want to share: how it began, what problems occurred, how it ended |
| **persuasive paragraph** | facts, figures, and examples to back up your opinion |
| **expository paragraph** | facts to explain the thing or process you're writing about |

**3** **Put the information in order.** The topic sentence is first. Next comes the body—the sentences that tell about the topic sentence. At the end is the closing sentence that sums up the paragraph, or tells what it means. (**SEE** pages 60-61.)

**4** **Check your work.** Read your paragraph. Imagine that you are reading it for the first time. Does it tell everything you need to know to understand the topic sentence? Is it interesting and clear?

# Details in a Paragraph

Details are an important part of any paragraph. They are the facts and examples that bring the paragraph to life.

## Personal Details

Most of the details you use in your paragraphs will be personal details—things you know from your own experience. Here are the different kinds of personal details you can use:

**Details from Your Senses** ● These details come from the world around you and are picked up by your five senses. They are things that you see, hear, smell, taste, and touch. You will need a lot of these when writing a descriptive paragraph.

**Details from Your Memory** ● These details come from memories of things you've done and experienced. In an expository paragraph, such details will help you to explain how to do something. In descriptive and narrative writing, they will help you to bring the past to life.

**Details from Your Imagination** ● These details come from inside your mind and deal with your hopes, wishes, and wonders. *What if Evan were a teacher?* Thoughts like this one can make narrative paragraphs interesting and fun.

## Details from Other Sources

When you write a paragraph, first think about what you already know about the subject. Then add details from other sources:

- ■ Ask people who may have the answers you need—teachers, parents, neighbors, friends.
- ■ Ask an expert on the subject. For example, if you are writing a paragraph about the flu that's going around, talk to a doctor or a nurse.
- ■ Check newspapers, magazines, and books. Check the ones you have at home and the ones in your library.

# Putting Things in Order

The sentences in the body of a paragraph must be organized so that the reader can follow the information from one sentence to the next.

**Time order.** It is easy to understand things that are explained in the order in which they happened. You may use words like *first, second, next,* and *finally.*

> **When** the fourth grade batted, Tim started off with a double. Jamie batted **next** and hit a home run. The fifth grade scored two runs in the third inning to tie the score. **After** Sarah hit a grand slam for the fourth grade in the next inning, the fifth grade never scored again.

**Place order.** When things are described in the order in which they are located, the description usually goes from left to right or from top to bottom. Place order can work well when you are writing a descriptive or an expository paragraph. Use words and phrases like **above, below, to the left of,** and **in front of** to guide your reader.

> **Looking at** the infield from home plate, the batter sees the third baseman on her far left. **To the right** of the third baseman is the shortstop. **To the right** of him is the second baseman, and **to the right** of her is the first baseman.

**Order of importance.** News stories are often organized this way. They tell the most important news first. Persuasive or expository paragraphs are also organized in this way, with the most important detail coming first *or* last.

> Very early this morning, an adult male ostrich escaped from the zoo. He was found about half a mile north of the zoo running along Adams Boulevard. Zoo officials say the ostrich was safely back in captivity within 15 minutes of his escape.

# Transition or Linking Words

**Words that can be used to show location:**

| | | | | |
|---|---|---|---|---|
| above | around | between | inside | outside |
| across | behind | by | into | over |
| against | below | down | near | throughout |
| along | beneath | in back of | off | to the right |
| among | beside | in front of | on top of | under |

**Words that can be used to show time:**

| | | | | |
|---|---|---|---|---|
| about | during | until | yesterday | finally |
| after | first | meanwhile | next | then |
| at | second | today | soon | as soon as |
| before | third | tomorrow | later | when |

**Words that can be used to compare two things:**

| | | |
|---|---|---|
| in the same way | likewise | as |
| similarly | like | also |

**Words that can be used to contrast things** (show differences):

| | | | |
|---|---|---|---|
| but | otherwise | on the other hand | although |
| yet | however | still | even though |

**Words that can be used to emphasize a point:**

| | | |
|---|---|---|
| again | for this reason | in fact |

**Words that can be used to add information:**

| | | | |
|---|---|---|---|
| again | and | for instance | as well |
| also | besides | next | along with |
| another | for example | finally | |

**Words that can be used to conclude or summarize:**

| | | |
|---|---|---|
| as a result | finally | in conclusion |
| therefore | lastly | in summary |

# Finding Paragraphs

You know how easy it is to go on and on when you have something important to say to one of your friends. "Guess what I did . . ." Well, the same thing can happen when you are writing about something that means a lot to you. You may start out writing a simple paragraph and end up filling a whole page or two with great ideas.

## Keeping Your Ideas Together

When your writing does go on and on, make sure it is organized into paragraphs before you share it. Otherwise, your readers may have trouble following your ideas. The guidelines that follow will help you find the paragraphs in your writing so that it is ready to be enjoyed.

*❝When I thought about my message, it became important for my readers to understand it.❞*

—Erik Olsen, student

## How You Do It

To find the paragraphs in longer pieces of writing, repeat these three steps—*Label, Name, Find*—until you come to the end of your work.

1. **Label:** Put a paragraph sign ( ¶ ) before the first word in your paper.
2. **Name:** Identify the first main idea in your writing.
3. **Find:** Locate the first sentence that is **not** about this idea.

\* \* \* \* \* \*

1. **Label:** Put a paragraph ( ¶ ) sign before this sentence (#3 above).
2. **Name:** Identify the main idea of this paragraph.
3. **Find:** Locate the first sentence that is **not** about this idea.

\* \* \* \* \* \*

1. **Label:** *Repeat the process until you are done.*

## Sample Writing

Here is part of an autobiography by student writer Elizabeth Hartfield. As you can see, it is not divided into paragraphs. (We took them out so you can see how the three-step process works.)

*My name is Elizabeth Frances Hartfield. I'm going to tell you about my life starting with the day something exciting and sad happened. What happened was that I moved from my home in Springfield to a house in West Chester. I was nervous and scared. I didn't think that I would make a lot of friends, but I did. Since I moved to West Chester, I have gone to three different schools. The first one I went to was Saints Simon and Jude. I went there for first and second grade. I went to Sacred Heart Academy in Bryn Mawr for third grade, and now I go to Villa Maria Academy. I am now in fourth grade. I like to draw a lot. On April 25, 1993, I won an award for a piece of artwork that I did. My favorite activities besides art are reading and dancing . . .*

## Following the Steps

Finding the paragraphs in this autobiography is easy if you follow the three-step process.

**1. Label:**   Put a paragraph sign ( ¶ ) next to the first word.
            ¶ *My name is . . .*

**2. Name:**   Identify the main idea of the first paragraph.
            *Moving to West Chester*

**3. Find:**   Locate the first sentence that is **not** about this idea.
            *Since I moved to . . .*

*   *   *   *   *   *

**1. Label:**   Put a paragraph sign before this sentence.
            ¶ *Since I moved to . . .*

**2. Name:**   Identify the main idea of this paragraph.
            *Different schools I've attended*

**3. Find:**   Locate the first sentence that is **not** about this idea.
            (See if you can find the last paragraph!)

# Writing Essays

## Think Before You Write!

Even if you've never written an essay before, you've probably thought out many of them. For example, if you've just read something interesting —maybe about saving trees—and decide to tell someone about it, you are "thinking" an essay. Or, if you're trying to figure out why you are such good friends with someone, you are also thinking an essay.

## Facts and Feelings

An essay is a form of factual writing that is more than one paragraph in length. Some essays are informational and sound like basic classroom reports. Other essays are freely written and include a lot of personal feelings. Most essays fall somewhere in between. They present a lot of good information about a specific subject, plus some of the writer's personal feelings.

The guidelines and model in this chapter will help you write a very basic informational essay—maybe your first essay ever! Good luck, and remember to think before you write.

# What an Essay Can Do

There are three basic reasons to write essays: *to present information, to share a strong opinion,* and *to make everyone think.*

## ➤ Present Information

If you want to present important facts and details about a subject, you can write an *informational essay.* In this type of writing, your goal is to inform your readers about something new or important. (An informational essay is like a classroom report, only shorter and not as detailed.)

*Subject Ideas:* **Reasons for Recycling Newspapers**
**Introducing a New Computer Game**

## ➤ Share a Strong Opinion

If you want to share an opinion about something going on in your school or community, you can write a *persuasive essay.* In this type of essay, your goal is to convince your readers to agree with your way of thinking. It's important that your opinion is supported by believable facts and details.

*Subject Ideas:* **Keeping the Buses Cleaner**
**Why a Computer Club Is Needed**

The most common type of persuasive essay is the letter to the editor. (**SEE** page 131 for an example. Also, see pages 308-311 for other helpful information.)

## ➤ Make Everyone Think

If you want to share your thoughts about a fun or serious subject related to your personal life, you can write a *personal essay.* Your goal is to entertain your readers, or to express your feelings about your subject.

*Subject Ideas:* **Fashion Trends with My Friends**
**Living with Allergies**

# Writing an Informational Essay

Writing an essay is no trouble at all if you know the **ins and outs** of the process.

**PREWRITING** *Getting Started*

To begin planning, answer three basic questions:

**Subject** ● Who or what am I writing about? (Make sure that your subject really interests you and that you already know something about it.)

**Audience** ● Who will be reading my essay? (Are you writing for your classmates, for another group of students, or for someone else?)

**Voice** ● How do I want my writing to sound? (Do you want to sound serious, funny, or somewhere in between?)

**PREWRITING** *Collecting and Organizing*

Next, decide on the type of information you plan to include:

**Explore** ● Write down all that you know about your subject.

**Focus** ● Review your writing, and decide what part of your subject you would like to cover. (For example, if your subject is recycling newspapers, you might focus on the ways it helps the environment.)

**Collect** ● Gather more information about your subject if you feel that you need to know more about it.

**Organize** ● Decide what details you are going to include in your essay and how they will be organized. (**SEE** page 77 for help.)

## WRITING THE FIRST DRAFT

When you are writing an essay, remember that each part—the beginning, the middle, and the ending—plays a special role:

**Beginning** ● Your first paragraph should say something interesting or surprising about your subject to get your readers' attention. It should also name the specific part of the subject that your essay will cover.

**Middle** ● The middle should include all of the ideas (facts, figures, examples) that support the subject. This information must be clearly organized. (This part may be more than one paragraph.)

**Ending** ● The final paragraph summarizes the main points covered in the essay. It should also remind readers why the subject is important, or help them remember it better.

## REVISING & EDITING

The following checklist will help you improve your first draft:

✔ Have I written a title that helps identify my subject?

✔ Have I introduced my subject in an effective way?

✔ Have I included enough facts and details to support my subject? Are they clearly stated?

✔ Will readers understand why my subject is important or interesting?

✔ Do I like the sound of my words and sentences? Have I checked for errors?

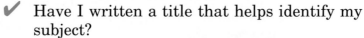

## Model Essay

The following informational essay deals with a very important subject, recycling. As you will see, all of the ideas are clearly stated and organized.

**Beginning**
A personal story introduces the subject.

**Middle**
Basic facts support the subject.

**Ending**
The main points are summarized.

### Why My Family Recycles Newspapers

In my family, we recycle our newspapers. My sister talked my parents into it after she studied recycling in school. I learned from her that old newspapers can be made into usable paper again. I also learned how recycling newspapers helps the environment.

There are three basic benefits when old paper is recycled. First, recycling saves trees. As more and more paper is recycled, fewer trees have to be used to make paper. Second, recycling saves energy. It takes less energy to recycle paper than to start the papermaking process by cutting down trees. Third, recycling old paper is cleaner than making paper in the old way. This means recycling causes less pollution.

It's easy to recycle old newspapers. We just put them in paper bags and drop them off at the recycling center every Saturday. It's worth the little time it takes because we are saving trees and energy and helping keep our air cleaner. Have you started recycling yet?

The question at the end of this essay will help readers remember the subject by encouraging them to start recycling, too.

# Organizing Your Essay

To help you organize the supporting facts and details in your essay, try *listing, clustering,* or *outlining.*

**Listing** ● For some essays, you can simply list the supporting details in the order you want to write about them.

- Recycling saves trees.
- Recycling saves energy.
- Recycling causes less pollution.

**Clustering/Webbing** ● When you have a lot of information, you may want to try a cluster or web. (**SEE** pages 26 and 222-223.)

**Outlining** ● Or, you may want to organize your ideas in an outline. An outline helps you arrange information from general to specific. A *topic outline* contains only words and phrases. (See the sample below.) You can also write a *sentence outline* if you want to add more detail.

## Sample Topic Outline

### Help for Blind People

I.  Help with reading and learning          ← Main Idea
    A.  Braille
    B.  Talking books          ← Examples
    C.  Enlarged-print books
        1.  Each letter enlarged by special machine
        2.  Readers feel large letters          ← Supporting Details
II. Help for moving about
    A.  Special walking cane
    B.  Trained dog
    C.  Sonar device

**YOU DON'T SSSSSAY**    In an outline, everything comes in pairs. If you have a *I,* you must have a *II.* If you have an *A,* you must have a *B,* and so on.

# A Writing Sampler

## Making Contact

All of the different *people, places, events,* and *objects* in your life have something special to offer you and your readers—if you take the time to write about them. You will see what I mean when you read the personal narratives and essays on the next five pages. They do more than just retell what happened to the writers. They show that the writers have carefully thought about their experiences and formed new ideas about them.

## Learning About Yourself

Writing about your personal experiences will help you practice storytelling. Part of becoming a good writer is being able to tell a good story. It will also help you understand that writing is much more than putting a few words on paper. You will learn that writing can be a very meaningful way to share, and even celebrate, special parts of your life.

> **"Writing from experiences is easy because I know all the details. Once I start, I can't stop."**
> —Mike Franzago, student

# Writing About a Special Person

Writing about another person is a very important form of writing. It is sometimes called biographical writing. A *biography* is the story of another person's life.

**Selecting a Subject** ● Write about someone you know well, or someone you would like to know well.

**Collecting Details** ● *List* details that describe your subject. *Remember* important things he or she has done. *Compare* your subject to other people. Who is he or she most like? *Ask* others about your subject, and *explain* why your subject is important.

## Student Model

Adam Garelick had a lot to say about his father in this story. His writing includes a lot of examples and real feelings.

**Beginning**
The writer introduces the subject.

**Middle**
One main activity is described.

**Ending**
Real feelings are expressed.

### Someone Who Cares

My dad is very special because he does so many things with me. He helps me with my homework, and if I ask him to take me somewhere, he'll do it. He even gives me confidence when I am having trouble with baseball.

My dad and I do so much together. Last summer, we took a trip across the country. We got to talk to each other a great deal. My dad told me about the time he was in the middle of nowhere and ran out of gas. After that story, I watched the gas gauge every other minute! He said he had made the same trip when he was 23 years old with his best friend. Now, it was him and me.

I wish everyone could have a companion like my dad. We all need an ally, or friend, in our lives; because if we have problems or need to express our feelings, we need a responsible person to turn to. I have my dad.

# Writing About a Special Place

Writing about a place is part descriptive writing and part narrative writing. You need to include details that describe your subject, but you also need to tell a good story about it.

**Selecting a Subject** ● Write about a place that has played an important role in your life. It can be a big place like a house you used to live in, or a small place like a certain tree in a yard.

**Collecting Details** ● If possible, *visit* this place, and *jot down* what you see, hear, smell, and feel. *Remember* personal experiences related to it. *Compare* your subject to other places. And *explain* what you like or dislike about it.

## Student Model

In this sample, Terra Wilcoxson remembers a special tree. She uses a lot of descriptive words and similes in her writing.

### It Was Tall and Mighty

**Beginning**
The writer remembers the tree.

Even though it lay on its side, it somehow seemed tall and mighty, like a friendly bear protecting me. When I climbed across it, nothing existed beyond the short range of the tree. My pudgy little hands could grasp branches that stuck out like spikes. I'd lift myself up and scamper across the trunk, afraid of plunging into the ditch of leaves below. When I finally reached the end, a sense of accomplishment and pride came over me.

**Middle**
The writer's feelings change.

Day after day passed, and I slowly drifted away, until my tree seemed to move into another dimension, isolated. Now it no longer stands tall or mighty. It just hangs there, like an old toy, forgotten.

**Ending**
Sadness is expressed.

Sometimes, I glance out the window at the weeping tree. It reminds me of all the hours I've spent climbing the bear it used to be.

# Writing About an Event

When writing about an event, make the action come alive for your readers, but don't try to say everything about your subject. It's better to focus on one exciting part of it. (**SEE** 110-115 for a related form of writing.)

**Selecting a Subject** ● Write about any recent event, or an event you plan to attend. For example, you may have attended a sporting event or a concert, watched a parade, and so on.

**Collecting Details** ● *Write down* all of the details related to your subject. Include sights, sounds, and smells. Also try to answer the 5 W's (*who? what? when? where?* and *why?*) related to it. Then *decide* why this event is worth sharing.

## Student Model

In this personal story, Michelle Diamond recalls the time she met her tennis idol. She makes this event sound very exciting.

**Beginning**
The writer wonders about meeting her idol.

**Middle**
The main activity is described.

**Ending**
The writer feels closer to her subject.

### The Unforgettable Autograph

I couldn't imagine really getting her autograph. What would it be like? I felt faint. She is my idol because at 14 she plays tennis so well. As she gets older, she will surely get even better.

While I was walking toward the practice courts, in my head I was hoping I would at least see her play. I was sure my sister was thinking the same thing. Then, suddenly, there she was, Jennifer Capriati, wearing her tennis jacket and listening to headphones. My sister and I ran over to her as fast as horses to a finish line. I stared at her with butterflies in my stomach. She actually signed my paper, and I felt like nothing else mattered.

Later, while I was watching her play, it might have been my imagination, but I thought she winked at me!

# Writing About a Special Object

When you write about an object, think of an interesting story to tell about it, a story that will help your readers know why this object is special to you. This is more important than describing the object in great detail.

**Selecting a Subject** ● Write about an object that you know well. You may have a special stuffed animal, a favorite baseball glove, a lucky charm, or a useful gadget of some type.

**Collecting Details** ● *List* details that describe the size, shape, and smell of your subject. *Remember* interesting stories related to the object. *Ask* yourself if your feelings about your subject have remained the same or have changed over time.

## Student Model

Michele Dreiding shares her feelings about an object that once played an important role in her life.

**Beginning**
The writer gives background information.

**Middle**
The story about the flashlight is told.

**Ending**
The ending ties into the title: "I'm Growing Up."

### I'm Growing Up

When I was little, I was scared of the dark. I thought monsters or ghosts would come out and yell "Boo!"

Finally, I got a flashlight, and that worked like a charm. It lit up my room a little so I could sleep better. Through the years, I enjoyed having my flashlight right next to my bed.

Now I am older, and I don't need it anymore. I no longer have a fear of the dark. Every time I take my flashlight out of the socket, my mom puts it back in again. I want to say, "Stop, Mom! I am growing up. I am not a baby anymore. You have to understand that I like the dark."

I know she is only trying to help, but . . .

# Writing About the Condition of Things

Some personal essays or stories are about the way things are, or about the *condition of things*. An essay about having allergies or about being too tall would fall into this category. In this type of writing, you share your feelings about a certain part of your life.

**Selecting a Subject** ● Write about some part of your life that makes you angry, happy, sad, or proud. You might write about wearing glasses, sharing a bedroom, or watching TV.

**Collecting Details** ● *Write down* all of your thoughts about your subject. If possible, *list* details that help answer *who? what? when? where?* and *why?* about the condition. Then *think* of the different ways this condition has affected your life.

## Student Model

In this essay, Christopher FitzSimons asks himself why he has to have allergies. A lot of honest feelings are expressed.

**Beginning**
The writer asks questions about his condition.

**Middle**
The questions continue.

**Ending**
The final lines are filled with emotion.

### Why?

Rachel has one problem—me. Wait. It's not me. It's my allergies! So why do I feel so guilty? Why do I think I'm shattering someone's dreams when my allergies are out of control? How come I feel like I've stabbed my sister in the heart when I can't stop my eyes from watering, tingling, itching?

Most of all, why do my allergies start right when everything is going so well, like when my family is about to buy a pet, or when we're playing with a kitten, or even when I'm watching my favorite TV show and I'm snuggled up in a warm, furry blanket.

I feel empty, like there's nothing inside of me, no love or compassion. I want to be in control, but I can't do anything about it.

Rachel can't get a cat because of me . . . me . . . ME!

# Improving Your Writing Skills

**Writing Basic Sentences**

**Combining Sentences**

**Writing with Style**

**Modeling the Masters**

**Writing Terms**

# Writing Basic Sentences

## Keeping Your Ideas Under Control

Let's say the tracking on Joe's VCR goes bonkers right in the middle of a good video. He tries everything, but the picture keeps jumping up and down like it has a bad case of hiccups. Finally, he gives up and turns off the machine.

Your readers may end up doing the same thing if your sentences seem out of control. If they can't follow your ideas, they will simply give up on your writing. That is why it is so important to use complete sentences. The guidelines in this chapter will help you write clear, correct sentences so that all of your ideas will be easy to follow.

*Always check your writing for sentence errors. This may be your most important job when you edit and proofread your work.*

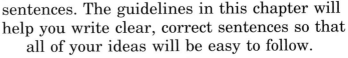

# SENTENCE REVIEW

Sentences are not hard to figure out. They are groups of words that express complete thoughts. You already know a sentence when you hear one because your mind is tuned in to complete thoughts. ***Your job as a writer is to listen carefully and write complete sentences.***

## The Basic Parts of a Sentence

All sentences have two basic parts—the subject and the verb.

**Subject** ● The subject usually tells us who or what is doing something.

*JOE watched his favorite video.*

**Verb** ● A verb expresses action or links the subject to another part of the sentence. (The verb is sometimes called the **predicate**.)

*Joe WATCHED his favorite video.* (action)

*He IS nuts about adventure movies.* (linking)

**Additional Words** ● Most sentences also contain additional words that describe or complete the thought.

*Joe watched HIS FAVORITE VIDEO.*

**Compound Subjects and Verbs** ● A sentence may include more than one subject or more than one verb.

*His MOM and BROTHER were in the kitchen.* (two subjects)

*Then the tracking WENT bonkers and RUINED Joe's fun.* (two verbs)

**Compound Sentence** ● Two sentences may be connected with *and*, *but*, or *or*.

*Later, Joe's mom fixed the tracking, AND he watched the video.*

 You can find more about sentences in the "Check It Out" section. (***SEE*** pages 370-373.)

# SENTENCE ERRORS

**Sentence Fragments** ● A **sentence fragment** is a group of words which does not express a complete thought. It is missing important information.

**Sentence Fragment:** *Thinks she is so cool.* (The subject is missing.)

**Corrected Sentence:** *Martha thinks she is so cool.*

**Sentence Fragment:** *Not cool to me.* (The subject and verb are both missing.)

**Corrected Sentence:** *She is not cool to me.*

**Run-On Sentences** ● A **run-on sentence** occurs when two sentences are joined without punctuation or a connecting word.

**Run-On Sentence:** *I thought the lopsided game would never end the score just kept getting worse and worse.* (Punctuation is needed.)

**Corrected Sentences:** *I thought the lopsided game would never end. The score just kept getting worse and worse.* (Punctuation has been added.)

**Corrected Sentence:** *I thought the lopsided game would never end, and the score just kept getting worse and worse.* (Punctuation and the connecting word *and* have been added.)

**Rambling Sentences** ● A **rambling sentence** happens when you put too many little sentences together with the word *and*.

**Rambling Sentence:** *I went skating down at the pond and three kids from my school were there and we fell on our fannies again and again and we laughed so much our stomachs hurt!* (Too many *and*'s are used.)

**Corrected Sentences:** *I went skating down at the pond, and three kids from my school were there. We fell on our fannies again and again. We laughed so much our stomachs hurt!*

# SENTENCE AGREEMENT

Make sure the parts of your sentence "agree" with one another. If you use a singular subject, use a singular verb; if you use a plural subject, use a plural verb. (Your subject and verb will then be in *agreement*.) The examples below will show you how this works.

## One Subject ● In most basic sentences, you have one subject
at the beginning of a sentence followed by the verb. Since they are often right next to each other, it is easy to check for subject/verb agreement.

> *Amy wants* **to go bowling.** (*Amy* and *wants* agree because they are both singular.)

> **Her** *parents want* **to go bowling, too.** (*Parents* and *want* agree because they are both plural.)

## Compound Subjects Connected by AND ● If a
sentence contains a compound subject connected by *and*, it needs a plural verb.

> *Harry and Earl spend* **most of their time teasing girls.**

> *Sarah and Jesse sing* **like squawking chickens.**

## Compound Subjects Connected by OR ● If a sentence
contains a compound subject connected by *or*, the verb must agree with the subject nearer to it.

> *Either the cat or the dog wakes* **me up each morning.**
>    (A singular verb is needed because *dog* is singular.)

> *Anna or her brothers feed* **the pets each evening.**
>    (A plural verb is needed because *brothers* is plural.)

**THINK IT OVER**

Sometimes the subject will not come at the beginning of the sentence. This will happen in questions and sentences beginning with the word *there*. Check these types of sentences very carefully for subject/verb agreement.

# SENTENCE PROBLEMS

Check your sentences for these problems:

**Double Subjects** ● Avoid sentences in which a pronoun is used immediately after the subject. The result is usually a double subject.

> **Double Subject:** *Some cats they eat all the time.* (The pronoun *they* should be omitted.)

**Corrected Sentence:** *Some cats eat all the time.*

**Pronoun/Antecedent Agreement** ● Make sure that the pronouns in your sentences agree with the words they replace. (These words are called antecedents.)

> **Agreement Problem:** *If my brother and his friend each eat three Big Macs, he will really be stuffed.* (The pronoun *he* is singular. The words it replaces—*my brother and his friend*—are plural.)

**Corrected Sentence:** *If my brother and his friend each eat three Big Macs, they will really be stuffed.* (Now the pronoun and the words it replaces agree; they are both plural.)

**Double Negatives** ● Do not use two negative words, like *never* and *no* or *not* and *no*, in the same sentence.

> **Double Negative:** *Never give no one a note in class.*

**Corrected Sentence:** *Never give anyone a note in class.*

> **Double Negative:** *I didn't have no mistakes in my paragraph.*

**Corrected Sentence:** *I didn't have any mistakes in my paragraph.*

**Confusing OF for HAVE** ● Do not use *of* in a sentence when you really mean *have*. (When *have* is said quickly, it sometimes sounds like *of*.)

> **Incorrect Usage:** *We should of won the game.*

**Corrected Sentence:** *We should have won the game.*

# Combining Sentences

## One Plus One Equals One

Sentence combining is making one smoother, more detailed sentence out of two or more shorter sentences. For instance, take a look at the following sentences:

*My dog loves to run fast.*
*He loves to jump fences.*
*He loves to chase rabbits.*

These three sentences are fine, but see what happens when they are combined. All of the ideas flow more smoothly.

*My dog loves to run fast, jump fences, and chase rabbits.*

The guidelines in this chapter will help you learn how to combine sentences. Learning this skill will help you write with more style.

**Sentence combining will come in handy when you are checking your writing for sentences that don't read smoothly.**

# Combining with a Key Word or Series

**Use a Key Word** ● Ideas from short sentences can be combined by moving a key word from one sentence to the other. This key word may be an adjective or an adverb.

Short sentences: *Kelly's necklace broke. It was beaded.*

■ *Combined sentence with an* **ADJECTIVE:**
   *Kelly's **beaded** necklace broke.*

Short sentences: *I am going to start my book report. I'll start it tomorrow.*

■ *Combined sentence with an* **ADVERB:**
   ***Tomorrow** I am going to start my book report.*

**Use a Series of Words** ● Ideas from short sentences can be combined into one sentence using a series of words or phrases.

Short sentences: *The gym teacher is strict. The gym teacher is organized. The gym teacher is fair.*

■ *Combined sentence with a* **SERIES OF WORDS:**
   *The gym teacher is **strict**, **organized**, and **fair**.*

 All of the words or phrases you use in a series should be *parallel*—stated in the same way. Otherwise, your sentences will sound like they are out of balance. (Look at the example below.)

Awkward series: *The dog was friendly, playful, and he was pretty smart, too.*

■ *Corrected sentence:*
   *The dog was friendly, playful, and smart.*

*Note:* This sentence is now correct because all the words in the series—friendly, playful, smart—are single-word adjectives. They are parallel.

# Combining with Phrases

**Use Phrases** ● Ideas
from short sentences
can be combined into
one sentence using
*prepositional* or
*appositive phrases.*
(***SEE*** pages 386 and 346.)

Short sentences: *Our cat curls up.*
*He curls up on top*
*of my homework.*

■ *Combined sentence with a* **PREPOSITIONAL PHRASE:**
   *Our cat curls up* on top of *my homework*

Short sentences: *Mrs. Keller makes the best cookies on the block.*
*Mrs. Keller is our next-door neighbor.*

■ *Combined sentence with an* **APPOSITIVE PHRASE:**
   *Mrs. Keller,* **our next-door neighbor,** *makes the best cookies on the*
   *block.*

## Use Compound Subjects and Compound Verbs ●

A compound subject includes two or more subjects in one sentence.
A compound verb includes two or more verbs in one sentence.

Two short sentences: *Tom danced around the room.*
*Mary danced around the room, too.*

■ *Combined sentence with a* **COMPOUND SUBJECT:**
   **Tom** and **Mary** *danced around the room.*

Two short sentences: *John slipped on the ice.*
*He fell on his rear end.*

■ *Combined sentence with a* **COMPOUND VERB:**
   *John* **slipped** *on the ice and* **fell** *on his rear end.*

# Combining with Longer Sentences

**Use Compound Sentences** ● A compound sentence is made up of two or more simple sentences joined together. The conjunctions *and, but, or, nor, for, so,* and *yet* are used to connect the simple sentences. (Place a comma before the conjunction.)

Two simple sentences: *My puppy has hair hanging over her eyes.*
*She looks just like a dust mop.*

■ *Combined sentence with* **AND:**
*My puppy has hair hanging over her eyes,* **and** *she looks just like a dust mop.*

Two simple sentences: *Our dog likes to eat shoes.*
*He won't touch my brother's smelly slippers.*

■ *Combined sentence with* **BUT:**
*Our dog likes to eat shoes,* **but** *he won't touch my brother's smelly slippers.*

**Use Complex Sentences** ● A complex sentence is made up of two ideas connected by words called subordinate conjunctions (*after, when, since, because, before,* etc.) and relative pronouns (*who, whose, which,* and *that*).

Two short sentences: *My best friend shares his lunch with me.*
*He doesn't like what his dad packs.*

■ *Combined sentence with* **BECAUSE:**
*My best friend shares his lunch with me* **because** *he doesn't like what his dad packs.*

Two short sentences: *Very cold weather closed school for a day.*
*The cold weather came down from northern Canada.*

■ *Combined sentence with* **WHICH:**
*Very cold weather,* **which** *came down from northern Canada, closed school for a day.*

# Writing with Style

## Learning by Doing

Style comes in many shapes and sizes. You may like to perform a certain stunt that gets you and your skateboard high off the ground. That's part of your own special style. You may like pepperoni on your pizza. That's also part of your style. You may like to wear your hair cut short or long or half-and-half. That's your style, too. What's *in style* for you depends on your own interests and tastes.

> **"**Writing isn't just words on paper anymore. It's me. **"**
> —Meredith Dempsey, student

## The Way You Write

As a young writer, you have your own special way of expressing your thoughts and feelings on paper. This is your writing style, and it will develop naturally as you write more and more. However, you can help your writing style along if you follow our suggestions in this chapter.

# Developing a Sense of Style

Your writing style will grow strong and healthy if you follow the advice listed below.

➤ **Practice often.** Keep a daily journal. This is the best way to develop your writing style.

➤ **Try different forms.** Write poems and riddles; write news stories and personal stories. Each form of writing has something special to offer you.

➤ **Write about ideas that are important to you.** If you write about subjects that really interest you, your writing style will have a better chance of developing.

➤ **Please yourself.** If you don't feel good about your writing, try again. Make it sound like the real you.

➤ **See how other writers do it.** When you read, look for sentences that read smoothly or contain eye-catching words. Write some of these sentences down. Then see if you can write your own sentences in the same way.

➤ **Write with details.** Writing without details is like baking cookies without flour. One of the most important ingredients is missing. Use details that help readers see, hear, smell, taste, and feel your subject. Also use similes (like the sentence about cookies) and metaphors.

➤ **Know when your writing doesn't work.** Watch for sentences that all sound the same as well as sentences that sound boring or lifeless. Then try to fix these!

MINI LESSON   This activity will help you write sentences with style. List five or six sentences from your writing (your best or your worst). Then try to change each sentence so it sounds better. You might change the order of the words in one sentence and use a different descriptive word in another one.

# Modeling the Masters

## Follow the Leaders

Beginning artists learn a lot about art by studying the work of famous painters. In the same way, you can learn a lot about writing by studying the work of your favorite authors. When you come across sentences or short passages that you especially like, practice building sentences of your own that follow an author's pattern of writing. This process is sometimes called "modeling." Here are some guidelines you can use for doing your own modeling.

## Guidelines for Modeling

- **Find** a sentence (or short passage) that you especially like.
- **Select** a subject for your copychange.
- **Follow** the pattern of your model sentences as you write about your subject.
- **Build** your sentence one small section at a time.
- **Review** your work, and change any parts that seem confusing or unclear.

# One Writer's Experience

## Modeling Roald Dahl

Kate has enjoyed Roald Dahl's stories for a long time, so every once in a while she tries to write like him. Here is one sentence from Dahl's book *Danny the Champion of the World*:

> ***Grown-ups are complicated creatures, full of quirks and secrets.***

Here's Kate's sentence, modeling Roald Dahl's sentence:

*Cats are complex beasts, going from lazy to crazy in no time.*

Kate might have written, "Some cats can be really nutty. They can go from being couch potatoes to crazy blurs of fur in no time." While this is fine, her modeling has taught her that she can create powerful ideas with fewer words. She has discovered a new pattern of writing.

## Modeling Will Hobbs

Later, Kate tried modeling a longer sentence from Will Hobbs's book *The Big Wander*. (This sentence describes the spooky sound made by a band of coyotes.)

> ***It wasn't but a second until the barks became yips and the yipping shifted into quavering sirens climbing higher and higher in pitch, as maybe a half-dozen coyotes harmonized like a band of lunatics and brought the hair rising on the back of his neck.***

Kate especially liked the sound of this sentence. She also liked the descriptive language it contained (*quavering sirens* and *coyotes harmonized like a band of lunatics*). Here's her sentence: (Notice that she is still thinking about her cat!)

*It wasn't but a minute until her paws became claws and the claws grew into slashing weapons, as a howling nightmare filled her head like a pack of mad dogs and made the fur on her back stand straight up on end.*

# Writing Terms

This list contains words used to describe different parts of the writing process. It also includes certain writing devices, or special ways of stating an idea.

**Anecdote** ● A brief story used to make a point. The story of young Abe Lincoln walking more than two miles to return several pennies to a customer is an anecdote which shows how honest Abe was.

**Arrangement** ● The way details are organized in writing. (**SEE** page 68 for more information.)

**Audience** ● Those people who read or hear what you have written.

**Body** ● The main part of the writing that comes between the opening and closing ideas. The body of a piece of writing contains the specific details that support or develop the main idea.

**Brainstorming** ● Collecting ideas in groups by freely sharing all of the different possibilities.

**Cliche** ● A familiar word or phrase which has been used so much that it is no longer a good way of saying something, such as *good as gold* or *bright as the sun*.

**Closing/Concluding sentence** ● The sentence which sums up the main point being made in a paragraph.

**Composition** ● Writing in which all the ideas work together to form a finished product.

**Conferencing** ● Working and sharing in writing groups.

**Description** ● Writing which paints a picture of a person, a place, a thing, or an idea using specific details.

**Details** ● The specific facts, examples, and words used in a piece of writing to support or explain the main idea.

**Diction** ● A writer's choice of words. In a story about everyday life, a writer may use very informal, everyday language. For a business letter, a writer will use more formal or proper language.

**Editing** ● Checking your writing to make sure the words and sentences are strong and smooth reading. Editing also means checking for spelling, grammar, and mechanics errors.

**Exaggeration** ● Words that stretch the truth. Exaggeration is used in tall tales: *The mosquito is so big it needs a runway to land.*

**Exposition** ● Writing which explains, such as a report or research paper. (Also called expository writing.)

**Figure of speech** ● A special way of writing to create an effective word picture. A figure of speech usually involves making a comparison of some type. (*SEE simile, metaphor,* and *personification.*)

**First draft** ● The first complete writing about a subject.

**Focus/Main idea** ● Concentrating on a specific part of a subject. When writing about a favorite person, you could focus on his or her sense of humor.

**Form** ● The shape of writing—a poem, an essay, a novel, a play, and so on. (*SEE* pages 34-35 for a complete list.)

**Free writing** ● Writing freely and rapidly to discover new ideas.

**Generalization** ● A statement which gives the general meaning rather than the specific details of a subject. "Writing helps you learn" is a generalization. (*SEE topic sentence.*)

**Grammar** ● The rules and guidelines of a language, which are used when you want to be correct in your writing and speaking.

**Irony** ● Using a word or phrase to mean the exact opposite of its normal meaning: Having the flu is *so much fun,* don't you think?

**Journal** ● A daily record of thoughts, feelings, and ideas.

**Limiting the subject** ● Narrowing a general writing subject to a more specific writing idea: *Pets—dogs—Labradors—older Labs—caring for older Labs.*

**Metaphor** ● A figure of speech that compares two different things without using a word of comparison such as *like* or *as: The streetlight was my security guard.*

**Modifier** ● A word, or group of words, which describes another word or idea. (*SEE* "Adjectives" and "Adverbs" on pages 384-385.)

**Narration** ● Writing which tells a story or recalls an experience.

**Objective** ● Writing which includes facts, with no opinions or personal feelings.

**Parallelism** ● The repeating of phrases or sentences that are written in the same way: Josie *scratched her head, bit her nails,* and *shrugged her shoulders.*

**Personal narrative** ● Writing which tells a story from the writer's life.

**Personification** ● A figure of speech in which an idea, object, or animal is given qualities of a person: *The rock refused to move.*

**Persuasion** ● Writing which is meant to change the way a reader thinks or acts.

**Prewriting** ● Planning a writing project. *Selecting a subject* and *collecting details* are prewriting activities.

**Process** ● A way of doing something which involves several steps; the writing process includes prewriting, writing the first draft, revising, editing and proofreading, and publishing.

**Proofreading** ● Checking a final draft for spelling, grammar, and mechanics errors.

**Prose** ● Regular writing in sentences and paragraphs.

**Pun** ● A word or phrase used in a way that gives it a funny twist: That story about rabbits is a real *hare raiser.*

**Purpose** ● The main reason a person has for writing.

**Revising** ● Changing a first draft to improve it.

**Sarcasm** ● Praise that actually means the opposite, and is meant to put someone down: That's *just great!*

**Sensory details** ● Details which help us to see, feel, smell, taste, and hear a subject.

**Simile** ● A figure of speech that makes a comparison using either *like* or *as*: *A gentle summer wind feels like a soft cotton sheet.*

**Slang** ● Special words and phrases used by friends when they are talking to each other. "Chill out" is a slang term.

**Style** ● A writer's choice of words, phrases, and sentences.

**Subjective** ● Writing which includes personal feelings.

**Supporting details** ● The details used to develop a subject or bring a story to life.

**Theme** ● The central idea or message in a piece of writing.

**Topic** ● The specific subject of a piece of writing.

**Topic sentence** ● The sentence which contains the main idea of a paragraph. (**SEE** pages 60-61.)

**Transitions** ● Words which help tie ideas together. (**SEE** page 69.)

**Voice** ● The way a writer expresses ideas. Writing that sounds believable is often written in an honest, natural voice.

# The Forms of Writing

# Personal Writing

**Writing in Journals**

**Writing Personal Narratives**

**Writing Friendly Letters**

# Writing in Journals

## Your Very Bad Day

Your old friend Bobbi Jones told everyone that your socks didn't match. Your mother packed you a cheese sandwich and two carrot sticks for the third day in a row. You never got a chance to bat during gym class. And on the way home from school, you left your favorite folder on the bus. Repeat after me: "It was a terrible, horrible, no-good, very bad day!"

How should you deal with a day like this? You could head straight for the Oreo cookies in the kitchen, "chill out" in front of the TV, or give your pillow a couple of body slams. But what happens when you can't look at another Oreo or watch another rerun? Your "very bad day" will still be there.

**Here's what I would do:** After a couple of cookies, I would get out my personal journal and write about all of the things that happened. Writing helps me sort out my thoughts. It helps keep me in control. It helps make bad days not seem so bad. And I almost always feel better when I'm done.

# Why Should You Write In a Personal Journal?

There are many reasons to write in a journal.  You can . . .

✔ **make notes of interesting things you see and hear,**
✔ **collect ideas for stories, poems, and reports,**
✔ **practice writing on your own,**
✔ **deal with your bad days,**
✔ **and relive all of your good times.**

## Here's how to get started . . .

**1** **Gather the right tools.** All you need is a notebook and some pens or pencils (or a computer).

**2** **Find a special time and place to write.**  Get up early in the morning and write while it is quiet in your house.  Write at a regular time during school.  Or plop down on your bed right after dinner and see how that works.

**3** **Write every day.** Write freely, exploring your thoughts and feelings as they come to mind.  Don't worry about what you say or how you say it.  Just keep writing for as long as you can (at least 5-10 minutes at a time).

**4** **Write about those things that are important to you.** Write about something that is bothering you or something you want to remember.  Write about what you did last weekend or something silly you saw.  Write about one thing and then later go on to something else.

**5** **Keep track of your writing.** Put the date on the top of the page each time you write.  Read through your journal writings from time to time.  Underline ideas you find interesting or surprising and ideas that you would like to write more about in the future.

# A Closer Look at Journal Writing

Journal writing works best when you can *reflect* or really think about your experiences and learn from them. When you can do this, your writing becomes more exciting—and full of surprises.

## ➤ *Reflect*

Thinking and writing in the following ways will help you explore and reflect upon your experiences.

**Ask questions:**  As you write, ask yourself some questions: *"What was fun or interesting about this experience?" "How do I feel about it now?"*  Or simply ask yourself *why?* at different points in your writing, and try to discover some answers.

**Wonder:**  Also think about what you have learned from an experience. *Compare* it to others you've had. *Wonder* what you could have done differently, or *predict* what the experience will mean to you in the future.

Read the model journal writing on page 108, and you will see that this student was writing and thinking (reflecting) about his father.

## ➤ *Push Yourself*

If you push yourself in your writing, you are sure to make some interesting discoveries.

**Keep it going:**  When you start a new journal writing, pick up right where you left off in your last entry. When you find an idea that surprises you, try to say more about it. When you think that you have said all that you can about a certain subject, keep going for at least a few more lines.

**Make connections:**  And if you want a challenge, try to make connections between ideas that seem really different. You can also make connections to events in the news, movies, songs, and so on.

# Kinds of Journals

If you enjoy exploring your thoughts in a personal journal, you might also enjoy writing in one of the special journals listed below.

**Dialogue Journal** ● In a dialogue journal, you and a friend, parent, or teacher write to each other about experiences you've had, books you've read, or ideas you wonder about. (**SEE** the sample on the next page.)

**Diary** ● A diary is a personal record of daily events as they happened. (You keep track of personal things in a diary.)

**Learning Log** ● In a learning log or class journal, you write about subjects like math and science to help you understand them better. (**SEE** pages 338-339 for more information.)

**Response Journal** ● Do you ever have strong feelings about the stories and books you read? You can write about these feelings in a response journal. (**SEE** page 137 for a list of writing ideas.)

**A Special-Event Journal** ● You may want to write about your experiences while participating in a sport, while preparing for a new member in the family, or while doing a special project.

## Sample Journal Writing

In the first sample, a student thinks and writes about his father and the army.

Oct. 26
I never imagined growing up without a father. He could have died in the Vietnam War. I never thought of it that way. I'm sure my mother did. The subject never comes up at home. But I think about my dad's military service a lot.
I wonder what I would do if I was in the army. Lt. Craven, it has a nice ring to it. Jogging 20 miles, 50 push-ups, and cheap food.
Just watching war movies I know what my father went through. I'm glad he's home, and everyone's happy . . .

## Dialogue Journal

In this second sample, a student and teacher carry on a conversation about a book.

Feb. 3

Dear Susan,

That part in <u>Mrs. Frankweiler</u> where the kids are hiding in the bathroom made me think of the time I hid from my mom in K-Mart. I didn't want to go home, so I hid behind the shower curtains. She was so mad! I thought of this because my heart was beating really fast whenever Mom got close to me, like the kids' hearts in the book. (Hey, when does your heart beat fast?)

Sincerely,
Mrs. N

Dear Mrs. N,

Thanks for your letter. You hid from your mother? That's funny. My heart beats fast (1) when we have spelling bees, (2) when I'm reading my book to the class, and (3) when you call on me to answer a math problem and I'm not sure where we are! (I have to number my problems!)

Your friend,
Susan

# Writing Personal Narratives

## The Stories of Your Life

Have you ever wished you could be the main character in a story? Well, guess what? You already are. You're the main character in the story of your life. A true story about yourself is sometimes called a **personal narrative**.

A personal narrative is a story about a personal memory. But it's not about any old memory. It's about a time so important you don't ever want to forget it.

## First Thoughts

Think about the different chapters (or experiences) in the story of your life. Some of them might make you laugh; some might make you shudder. Then again, maybe some of them make you feel angry or happy or sad or excited. Any experience that has caused you to feel a strong emotion is a good subject for a personal narrative.

> 66 **It's not easy to travel back into your memory and gather details. But it's worth it. They help your reader understand what happened. And they help you remember the very important chapters in the story of your life.** 99
> —Sandy Asher

## Model Personal Narrative

Here's a true story about me and my family. When it happened, I felt scared, sad, and then happy. (I'm sure you have plenty of your own exciting stories to share.)

### THE GREAT GERBIL ESCAPE

When my daughter Emily was nine years old, she had a pair of gerbils named Farrah and Festus. One day, Festus escaped from our bathtub!

It sounds silly to have gerbils in your tub, but it's not. The sides are too high to jump over and too slick to climb. We plugged the drain. We put in toys and sunflower seeds. The gerbils could exercise and play safely.

But one day, I accidentally left a fuzzy blue bath mat over the edge of the tub. When Emily and I came back, Festus was gone. He'd grabbed the mat and climbed out!

The only place he could have gone was down the heat vent in the wall. We knelt beside the vent. We could hear him! "Scritch-scratch. Scritch-scratch." We lowered a rope into the vent, but he didn't climb out. We stuffed in a towel, but he didn't climb that either.

And when we pulled the towel out, there was no more "Scritch-scratch." Oh, no! I thought. We've pushed him down the vent into the furnace. We've baked our gerbil!

Emily was heartbroken. I felt terrible. We put Farrah back in the cage and went downstairs. Then I noticed another heat vent in the hall, right below the one upstairs in the bathroom. And sure enough, we could hear Festus again: "Scritch-scratch. Scritch-scratch!"

Finally, Emily remembered that gerbils love to explore boxes. We took all the tissues out of a small tissue box. Emily lowered the box into the vent as far as her arm could reach. Then Festus climbed aboard and rode to safety in his own private elevator. And that's how the Great Gerbil Escape became the Great Gerbil Rescue!

The story is organized according to time (describing what happens first, second, third, and so on).

Each new action adds suspense and interest to the story.

# Gathering Story Ideas

You can start gathering ideas for personal narratives by writing in a daily diary or journal, or by making lists of personal experiences. A good way to find ideas is to ask yourself the following types of questions:

## ■ Who are the important people in your life?

Family members? Friends? Classmates? Neighbors? Think about the times you've shared with each one. What do you remember best? What would you just as soon forget?

## ■ Where have you been?

Every place you visit is an adventure, whether it's the doctor's office, the principal's office, or Disneyland. Think of the biggest place you've been, and the smallest. Think of comfortable places, and places that cause you to squirm. Think of special meeting places from your past.

## ■ What do you like to do?

Do you enjoy drawing or cooking or caring for animals? Do you like to play ball or just hang out? Do you like to talk on the phone or read at night when you're supposed to be asleep?

## ■ What do you *not* like to do?

Study? Clean your room? Babysit? Get up early? There are a lot of ways to answer this question, aren't there? And a lot of strong feelings involved, too. Isn't it nice to know that even the *worst* times you can remember are at least good for story ideas?

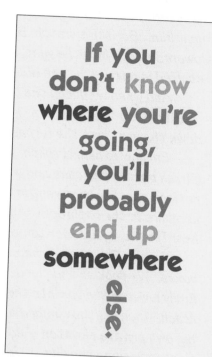

**If you don't know where you're going, you'll probably end up somewhere else.**

# Writing a Personal Narrative

## PREWRITING  *Planning Your Way*

**Select a Subject** ● Choosing a subject for a personal narrative should be easy. You're looking for a memorable experience that happened over a short period of time. (**SEE** "Gathering Story Ideas" on the previous page for help.)

**Collect Your Thoughts** ● If the experience you select seems really clear in your mind, go right to your first draft. Write it all out as best you can. If you're a little fuzzy about all of the details, try doing a cluster or making a list.

As soon as you can answer the 5 W's—*Who? What? When? Where?* and *Why?*—about the experience, you're probably ready to write.

## WRITING THE FIRST DRAFT

**Start at the Beginning** ● Put yourself at the beginning of the experience ("There I stood" or "As I entered the room") and continue to add details as they come to mind. Don't worry about saying everything. You can fill in any gaps later when you revise.

## REVISING  *Improving Your Writing*

**Review Your Work** ● Look over your first draft. Have you left out any important details, or put things in the wrong order? Ask a classmate to review your writing as well. Then make the necessary changes in your story. (**SEE** "Striking It Rich in Your Story" on page 114 for helpful writing reminders.)

## EDITING & PROOFREADING

**Check for Careless Errors** ● Make sure that your writing makes sense and reads smoothly. Then write a neat, error-free final draft and proofread it.

# Striking It Rich in Your Story

Here are some special reminders to help you develop your personal narrative:

**Add Physical Details** ● Take another look at my gerbil story. Can you see what I saw? There are two gerbils in the tub, with its high, slick sides. There's the fuzzy blue bath mat and the heat vent in the wall. It's important that you help your readers see the details that matter. You do this by adding important facts and by leaving out facts that are less important to your story.

**Add Sounds, Tastes, Smells, and Textures** ● Sounds make readers feel as if they were there, living the adventure with you. I emphasize one important sound in my story: "Scritch-scratch!" What about taste, smell, and touch? Did I include all of those in my gerbil tale? Only touch. I mentioned that the tub was slick and the bath mat was fuzzy. Taste and smell weren't important in my story, but they might be in yours.

**Add Dialogue** ● Dialogue always makes a story seem real. Here's how I might have started my story with dialogue:

> "Mom, look!" Emily shouted.
> "Festus is gone!"
>
> "Gone?" I asked, rushing into the
> bathroom after her. "What do you mean?"

**Add Thoughts and Feelings** ● What helped you understand my thoughts and feelings in "The Great Gerbil Escape"? Comments like "Oh, no!" and "I felt terrible" surely helped. A narrative without the writer's thoughts and feelings would not have that special personal touch that can make this type of writing so much fun to read.

 **TAKE NOTE** Write the way you feel. If your subject makes you laugh, try to make your readers laugh. Or, if your subject makes you feel sad or excited, try to make your readers feel the same way.

## Student Model

In this model narrative, Jessica Gilbert recalls a motorcycle ride that taught her an important lesson.

### When I Got Burned on My Dad's Motorcycle

As I was going outside, I was happy because I was going to ride on my dad's motorcycle. It was always fun.

"Come on. Get up," said my dad cheerfully.

"Okay," I answered. But just as I was getting onto the seat, I burnt myself on one of the accelerator pipes!

"Ow!" I yelled as I started to cry.

"Are you all right?" asked my mom.

"No," I answered.

"Come here," said my mom. "Let's take a look at that burn. It's really bad. I don't think she should go for a ride on the motorcycle."

I felt really glad that my mom had said that.

"Aw, come on. It won't hurt her anymore than she's already hurtin'," said my dad. I started to get really angry. I mean, I was only five years old. I hurt! Why should I have to ride the motorcycle?

Then he picked me up and set me on the seat of the motorcycle.

"Dad, I don't wanna go!" I said, still crying.

"Nonsense. Now stop crying," said my dad. And we took off.

I have to admit that during the ride, I started to laugh. My burn hardly hurt anymore. I was still sniffling a little when we got back, but it had been a fun ride.

I'm really glad my dad made me get on the motorcycle. If he hadn't, I probably never would have gotten on it again. From that day on, I knew I would never give up after I got hurt. I would just get back up and try it again.

*Dialogue makes the story seem real.*

*The writer shares her thoughts and feelings with the reader.*

# Writing Friendly Letters

## Keeping in Touch

Do you ever run to the mailbox to see if anything is addressed to you? Everyone enjoys receiving mail, especially letters. Letters from friends make friendships stronger. Letters from relatives make you feel closer. The best way to make sure you receive a letter is to send one.

### Parts of a Friendly Letter

Friendly letters have five parts: the *heading*, the *salutation*, the *body*, the *closing*, and the *signature*.

➤ The **heading** includes your address and the date. Write it in the upper right-hand corner.

➤ The **salutation** or greeting usually begins with the word *Dear* and is followed by the name of the person who will receive the letter. Place a comma after the name. Write a salutation at the left-hand margin, two lines below the heading.

➤ The **body** of the letter contains your thoughts and ideas. Begin writing on the second line after the salutation. Keep the paragraphs short for easy reading.

➤ Write the **closing** two lines below the body of your letter. Capitalize only the first word and follow it with a comma. Put your **signature** under the closing.

## Model Friendly Letter

Tracy introduced herself in this letter to her new pen pal, Grace.

**Heading**

123 Wixom Road
Wixom, MI 48386
January 8, 1994

**Salutation**

Dear Grace,

My name is Tracy, and I am your new pen pal. I'm in the fifth grade at Wixom Elementary School in Wixom, Michigan.

I'll start by telling you about some of my hobbies. I am taking keyboard lessons because I got a keyboard for Christmas, and I think it will be fun. I'm not very good, yet, but I can play two songs. Have you ever played a keyboard?

Another hobby of mine is horseback riding. Have you ever been horseback riding? When my dad was 15, besides school, he worked at a horse ranch. I think that is neat.

**Body**

I really like to draw, paint, and read stories. I also love to read mystery books and fiction books. My favorite mystery series is Nancy Drew. Do you like to read?

I have three people in my family: my mom, my dad, and me. My mom is in advertising, and my dad is in sales. I also have ten pets: seven fish, two parakeets, and a dog. My dog's name is Hershey. My family and I named her that because she's all brown, like a Hershey's chocolate bar. My two birds, Sammy and Tweedy, are green, blue, yellow, and black. Tweedy bites, and because of that, it's really hard to train her. Sammy is trained and can ride on my shoulder in the house.

As you probably have noticed, I love animals. I want to work with animals when I grow up, especially with whales. What do you want to be when you grow up?

**Closing**

Sincerely,

**Signature**

Tracy Randlett

P.S. Write back soon!

# Writing a Friendly Letter

**PREWRITING** *Planning Your Letter*

**Choose a Friend** ● This part is easy! Write to someone who wrote to you, someone you haven't seen in a long time, or a special person you want to talk to in a letter. Maybe you'd like to have a pen pal as Tracy did.

**Gather Ideas** ● List all of the ideas you want to include in your letter. Gather all the details you will need to make each idea clear. Here are some ideas to get you started:

- ■ Share a good story.
- ■ Tell what's been on your mind.
- ■ Describe something you like to do.
- ■ Tell about the latest book you've read.
- ■ Share a favorite poem, or write one of your own.
- ■ Provide a few questions for your friend to answer.

**WRITING**

**Get Started** ● Begin by telling all about one of the ideas on your list. Any one will do! Tracy started by telling all about her hobbies and the things she likes to do. Then she told about her family and pets.

**Write Back** ● If you are writing back to a friend, you can start by answering the questions he or she may have asked. Then add the new information about yourself.

**THINK IT OVER**

Writing a friendly letter gives you a chance to think about your own life. In this way, you benefit from writing a letter as much as the person who receives it.

## REVISING  *Improving Your Letter*

Try to make your letter easy to read and entertaining. Read the sentences over to be sure they make sense. Remember to start a new paragraph each time you switch to a new story or idea.

## EDITING & PROOFREADING

Check your letter for spelling, punctuation, and capitalization. Also check the form of your letter, especially if you are writing to someone who is not a close friend or relative. Then neatly write or type a final copy if you need to. A correctly written letter will make a good first impression.

**P.S.** If you have already finished your letter and then remember something you forgot to say, add a P.S. (postscript) at the bottom under your signature.

# Address the Envelope

Address the envelope clearly and correctly so it is sure to reach its destination. Also make sure to fold your letter so that it fits neatly into the envelope. (**SEE** page 146.)

Miss Tracy Randlett
123 Wixom Rd.
Wixom, MI   48386

Miss Grace Jackson
682 State St.
Springfield, IL   62704

# Writing Social Notes

Sometimes you will need to write a special kind of friendly letter—a thank-you note or an invitation. These are often called **social notes**.

## Parts of Social Notes

A social note begins with a **salutation** (*Dear _____ ,*). The middle of your note, the **body**, is usually one or two paragraphs. The paragraphs are short and to the point. "Your friend" or "Love" are common **closings**. Don't forget to sign your note with your **signature**.

**Invitations** ➤ When you are inviting someone to come to a party or special event, you'll need to write an **invitation**. Be sure to include these items:

- *What:*  a party, a celebration
- *When:*  the date and time
- *Where:*  the place and address
- *Who:*  who the party is for
- *Why:*  birthday, bar mitzvah, going away

Ask for an answer in your letter if you want to know whether or not the person will be coming to your event. You can also add R.S.V.P. and your telephone number in the lower left-hand corner.

**Thank-You Notes** ➤ When writing a *thank-you note*, be specific. If you are thanking someone for something special he or she did, explain why it was important to you. If you are thanking someone for a gift, tell why you like it and how you are using it.

**Bright IDEA**

You can make your own customized notes and invitations with rubber stamps, watercolors, colored markers, stickers, special lettering, etc. Be creative!

## Sample Invitation

Dear Josh,

My tenth birthday is coming up, and my dad said I could have a party. He's going to take us to the zoo, and the director said we could go on a scavenger hunt.

The party will be on my birthday, April 29th. You can be dropped off at 12:30 and picked up at 4:00 p.m.

My address is 3200 North Main Street. Bring a raincoat if it looks like rain. Please call me to let me know if you can come.

Anna
R.S.V.P. 639-2231

## Sample Thank-You Note

THANK YOU
THANK YOU
THANK YOU
THANK YOU
THANK YOU
THANK YOU
THANK YOU
THANK YOU
THANK YOU
THANK YOU
THANK YOU
THANK YOU
THANK YOU

Dear Josh,

Thanks for coming to my party. The book and paper-making kit you gave me are great. I started reading 50 Simple Things Kids Can Do to Save the Earth, and I'm already working on some of the ideas.

I started collecting junk mail to use for the paper-making kit. I'll show you how my first paper turns out. Thank you very much for the presents. I really like them.

Your friend,
Anna

# Subject Writing

**Writing Newspaper Stories**

**Writing Book Reviews**

**Writing Explanations**

**Writing Business Letters**

**Writing Observation Reports**

# Writing Newspaper Stories

## Look!
## Up in the Sky!
## It's a Reporter!

How would you like to be Superman for a day? Would you like to zoom through the sky? Leap over tall buildings? Discover secrets with your X-ray vision?

You may remember that Superman, when he wasn't flying around in his long underwear, had a real job. As Clark Kent, he worked as a newspaper reporter.

## Real-Life Reporters

Some reporters think that writing stories about important events and memorable people is more interesting than being a comic-book hero. As you read this chapter, maybe you'll see why.

> *Starting today, you can be a reporter in your own classroom, school, and community. All you need is a little curiosity, an interest in people, and, of course, a reporter's notebook! With a little energy and creativity, you can even produce your own newspaper.*
> —Roy Peter Clark

# The Parts of a Reporter

A curious mind to think of story ideas

Eyes to see interesting details

Ears to listen for good quotes

A nose for news

A mouth to ask the right questions

Heart to understand people

Feet for following up on good stories

Hands for writing down good notes

# Interviewing

Many wonderful stories result from interviews.  During an interview, the reporter asks people questions about their experiences. The result can be a dramatic and funny adventure, like this one:

### JAWS!
*By Karin Fraser*

One day last summer during school vacation, a boy named Billy Shannon was at the Don CeSar Beach.  He was swimming in the Gulf of Mexico.  He was swimming near the deep water markers, and he felt something rubbery slide against his leg and saw a fin.

He called "Help!" about four or five times.   A few people went out of the water.  The movie <u>Jaws</u> flashed through his mind.  The lifeguard went to him in a jet-ski. He pointed out that they were dolphins.

Billy swam back to the shore.  He went to the pool where his parents were.  He was quite embarrassed.  He told them the story, and they thought it was funny.  His brother made fun of him, and Billy punched him in the jaw.

## Tips for Interviewing

✔ Prepare a list of questions beforehand.

✔ Start with a question from your list, but then try to make the interview seem like a *real* conversation.

✔ Listen carefully, write quickly.

✔ When you take notes, politely say, "I want to write that down."  The person will stop so you can write.

✔ Ask the person to spell any names you're unsure of.

✔ Remember that **the meaning is more important than the exact words**.

# Finding News Stories

A news story tells readers about an important or unusual event. The more important the event, the more interesting the news. An old joke says that when a dog bites a man, it is not news. But when a man bites a dog, that's news!

The headlines below show the difference between news that is news, and news that is not news.

**News:**

> Daily Chronicle
> ## Class Makes Flying Saucer

**Not News:**

> Daily Chronicle
> ## Saucer Breaks in Cafeteria

**News:**

> Daily Chronicle
> ## Flu Hits Jones School

**Not News:**

> Daily Chronicle
> ## Student Gets Headache

**News:**

> Daily Chronicle
> ## Artists Receive Awards

**Not News:**

> Daily Chronicle
> ## Art Teacher Draws in Class

MINI LESSON  Newspaper stories are about real events, not make-believe ones. Make a list of interesting things that have recently happened at your school. Put stars next to the ones that you think would make good news stories.

# Three Types of Stories

Here is a list of stories written by students in St. Petersburg, Florida. They decided to name their classroom newspaper the *Cougar Chronicle*, after the school mascot. The newspaper's motto is "If a fifth-grader needs to know it, we print it." You will notice that these stories are listed under three general story types: news stories, human interest stories, and opinion letters to the editor.

## News Stories

- A power outage kills fish in the fifth-grade aquarium.
- Swimmer Nicole Haislett, who lives nearby, wins a Gold Medal in the Olympics.

## Human Interest Stories

- What is it like to see a baby being born?
- Who is the fastest reader in third grade?
- Our math teacher plays in a rock band.
- Your friend mistakes a dolphin for a shark. (**SEE** "Jaws!" on page 125.)

## Opinion Letters to the Editor

- There should be a greater variety of nutritious foods in the school cafeteria.
- We should have more time for reading and more books available in our classroom.
- People should not give pets as gifts because the pets are often abandoned.

THINK
About It

A good reporter sees the world as a storehouse of story ideas. Look around, be curious, read, and ask questions. You'll discover stories everywhere—in your classroom, school, and community—enough to fill up the pages of any classroom newspaper.

## Daily Chronicle

**❶ Lakewood Girls Win Soccer Championship!**

❷ by Anna Flanagan

The girls of Lakewood High School made history yesterday. They became the first West ❸ Florida team to win a state soccer championship. They beat Rockledge High by a score of 1-0.

"The girls played great," said ❹ Coach Bill Carter. "I'll always remember this team. In my eyes they were all stars."

❺ Ever since Susan James broke the team record by scoring five goals against Central, no one could stop Lakewood. Susan and her teammates, Darcy Smith and Colleen Kelly, played such good defense that only one goal was scored against them in their last three games.

They have set a new record for their high school, ending the season with a record of 7 wins and 0 losses.

❻ Coach Carter smiled as he said, "Eight members of our soccer team will return next year. I am ready for the season to start right now."

## Parts of a Newspaper Story

❶ The **Headline** is a title that tells the story in bold type:
**Lakewood Girls Win Soccer Championship!**

❷ The **Byline** gives the writer credit for the story.

❸ The **Lead** tells the reader the most important news:
*"The girls of Lakewood High School made history yesterday. They became the first West Florida team to win a state soccer championship. They beat Rockledge High by a score of 1-0."*

❹ A good **Quote** gives life to a story:
*"The girls played great," said Coach Bill Carter. "I'll always remember this team."*

❺ The **Body** of the story answers questions for the reader:
- Who played well?
- How many games has the team won this season?

❻ The **Ending** gives the reader something to remember:
*"Eight members of our soccer team will return next year. I am ready for the season to start right now."*

# Writing a News Story

**PREWRITING** *Planning Your Writing*

**Select a Subject** ● Write about a *newsworthy* subject—something important, interesting, or unusual that your readers will want to read about.

**Collect Details** ● You can do this by interviewing people, making eyewitness observations, and so on. A good starting point is to ask the 5 W's and H—*Who? What? Where? When? Why?* and *How?* (Try to include enough information to answer any questions your readers may have.)

## WRITING THE FIRST DRAFT

**Write the Lead or First Paragraph** ● Begin with the most important or interesting detail. If at all possible, put a person in the lead paragraph—for example, a baker spinning a pizza crust, or a lifeguard hearing a shout for help. (**SEE** page 130.)

**Write the Main Part of Your Story** ● Remember that the most important information is usually stated early in basic news stories. Try to leave your readers with something to think about in the ending.

**REVISING** *Improving Your Writing*

**Review Your Work** ● Make sure you have included all of the important facts and details in your story. Also make sure your information is correct and in the best possible order.

## EDITING & PROOFREADING

**Check for Careless Errors** ● Pay careful attention to the spelling of names! Have your teacher or a classmate review your work as well. Write the final copy of your story.

# Writing a Lead

The beginning of a newspaper story is called a **lead** because it leads the reader into the rest of the story. The lead can be a short sentence or a paragraph. When it is well written, the lead pulls the reader into the story, and prepares the reader for what comes next.

Remember Karin Fraser's lead for the story "Jaws!"? She begins the story with a bit of danger, so the reader will want to find out if Billy Shannon is going to be the victim of a shark attack.

## Student Models

Here are some leads written by student reporters. Read them and then imagine what the rest of the story will be about:

*I rode six hours in a little yellow Datsun, but it was worth it. I finally got to see the greatest concert in years.*

*Picture in your mind the most beautiful sunset you've ever seen, the one sunset that you'll remember forever.*

*Everybody was in uniform, out on the field, and ready for the final game of the season.*

*Tommy Walton is "The World's Greatest Singing Hot-Dog Salesman," a 58-year-old man with the heart and soul of a teenager.*

## Lead Sampler

The samples listed here will help you write leads for human interest stories.

■ **Question Lead:** *Have you ever watched a true hot-dog lover in action?*

■ **Suspense Lead:** *Should she hold the pickle relish or mustard? Tanya Robinson couldn't decide.*

■ **Surprise Lead:** *A dog with the works is worth the indigestion.*

# Writing a Letter to the Editor

As a citizen of the United States, you have many rights and freedoms. Americans benefit from freedom of religion, freedom of expression, and freedom of the press. One way to practice your freedom is to write a letter to the editor of a newspaper.

BUDDY SNIDER
1715 PALM ST
ST PETERSBURG FL 33712

LETTERS TO THE EDITOR
THE COUGAR CHRONICLE
BOX 1101
ST PETERSBURG FL 33712

1715 Palm St.
St. Petersburg, FL 3
October 15, 1993

Editor
The Cougar Chronicle
Box 1101
St. Petersburg, FL 33712

Dear Editor:

During the last six years that I have been going to Bay Point Elementary School, the lunches have been getting smaller, and the prices have been getting bigger! I have noticed that the little mustard and ketchup containers have taken one whole space on the tray that used to be filled with a vegetable or something else.

We are also getting smaller main courses. When I get home from school, I eat a lot; and sometimes my mom has to tell me to stop.

Maybe it is because I'm getting older and I eat more, but I think that the school lunches are getting smaller.

Yours truly,

*Buddy Snider*
Buddy Snider

◀ **Here is a student's letter:**

Good newspapers will publish letters written by young people. They know that young writers have strongly felt beliefs and that their opinions are important.

# Writing Book Reviews

## Sharing Your Views

The students in one elementary classroom in Troy, Michigan, really enjoy sharing their thoughts and feelings in book reviews. Their classroom is loaded with books to choose from. And after reading each other's reviews, the students always know which books they want to read next.

**In a book review you share your understanding of and opinion about a book you have read.**

## Becoming an Expert

The students also enjoy this form of writing because it gives them a chance to write about subjects that really interest them. For example, two students named Devon and Christa are both crazy about sports. When they read good sports stories, they *want* to write about them. And when other students want to read sports stories, they turn to Devon and Christa (and their reviews) for suggestions.

## Model Book Review

In the following model, student writer Hilary Ormond reviews the book *The True Confessions of Charlotte Doyle* by Avi. Each paragraph in this model answers one of three basic questions: *What is the book about? What is the book's theme or message? What do I like about this book?*

### The True Confessions of Charlotte Doyle

**What is the book about?**

<u>The True Confessions of Charlotte Doyle</u> is about a wealthy thirteen-year-old girl named Charlotte. In 1832, Charlotte is supposed to sail from England to Rhode Island with two other families, but the families never show up. Charlotte decides to sail with the crew alone. She becomes good friends with the captain, until the captain kills two of the crewmen for being traitors. Charlotte then decides to join the crew and becomes "Mr. Doyle" in the logbook. During a storm, the first mate, Hollybrass, is killed with her knife!

**What is the book's theme or message?**

I think Avi, the author, wanted to tell his readers that even people like Charlotte who are very shy can become strong and brave. She had to make many hard choices. I think he also wanted readers to understand that accusations aren't always true.

**What do I like about this book?**

I liked the book because Avi made all the characters seem real. It was well written and full of imagination and suspense. I wanted to know what would become of Charlotte Doyle, so I read into the night to get my answer.

Readers don't have to know everything that happens in your book, or all of your reasons for liking it. Try to say enough so they can decide if they want to read it themselves.

# Writing a Book Review

## PREWRITING  *Planning Your Review*

**Select a Subject** ● The type of book you review is really up to you. It could be a mystery, or an adventure story, or maybe a new book about your favorite sports figure. Just make sure that you enjoyed the book, or that you have strong feelings about it.

**Collect Your Thoughts** ● Your book review should answer three basic questions: *What is the book about? What do I like about the book? What is the book's theme or message?* (The "Collection Sheet" on the next page will help you gather information.)

## WRITING THE FIRST DRAFT

**Include the Right Stuff** ● The first paragraph in your review should give the name and author of your book, and also answer the "What is the book about?" question. The other two questions should be answered in separate paragraphs.

## REVISING  *Improving Your Writing*

**Make It Clear** ● Carefully review your first draft, checking for ideas that seem unclear or out of order. Also make sure that no paragraph says too much or too little. Saying too much can sometimes be a problem, especially in the first paragraph.

## EDITING & PROOFREADING

**Check It Out** ● Make sure your review reads clearly from start to finish. Also check for spelling and punctuation errors. (Remember that titles should be underlined.) Then write a neat final draft and proofread it.

# Collection Sheet

The ideas listed below will help you form answers for the three basic review questions. (Notice that there are separate ideas for fiction and nonfiction books.)

**1.  What is the book about?**

*Fiction:* *What events happen in the story?* (A book review should highlight a few events rather than give the whole story away.)

*Nonfiction:* *What is the basic subject of this book?  Is there one part of the book that seems really important?*

**2.  What do I like about the book?**

*Fiction:* *Does the book start in an exciting or interesting way?  Does the book contain a lot of action or suspense?  Does the main character show courage or strength?  Does the book end in a surprising way?*

*Nonfiction:* *Does the book contain interesting information?  Is the information easy to follow?  Does the book contain colorful illustrations?*

**3.  What is the book's theme?**

*Fiction:* *What message about life is the author trying to make?* (Here is a sample message: It's not easy to stand up for your rights.) *How do you know that this is the message?*

*Nonfiction:* *Why do you think the author wrote this book? What basic information or message does the author want to share?*

**YOU DON'T** sss**SAY**

As you collect your ideas, you can write possible answers to each question on separate index cards.

# A Review with a Special Focus

Another way to write a book review is to give it a special focus. Writer Heather Monkmeyer feels that *The True Confessions of Charlotte Doyle* is a very suspenseful book. As you will see, this feeling of suspense ties all of her ideas together. It is the focus of her review.

---

### The True Confessions of Charlotte Doyle

The first paragraph tells what the "focus" of the review is.

"Not every thirteen-year-old girl is accused of murder, brought to trial, and found guilty. But I was such a girl. . . ." That is the opening line of The True Confessions of Charlotte Doyle by Avi. From the first line to the final paragraph, Avi creates suspense by telling just enough to make readers ask questions that need good answers.

In the first chapters, Avi creates suspense by setting up strange circumstances. As Charlotte boards the ship that will take her to America, she learns that she is the only passenger. That really made me begin to wonder.

Three suspenseful events are highlighted.

Sometimes Avi creates suspense by the things Charlotte does. She tries to stop the captain from killing an innocent man and slashes the captain's face in the process. What will the captain do to her?

Avi packs in a double helping of suspense when the cruel captain sentences Charlotte to be hanged for a murder she did not commit, while at the same time, the crew turns against her.

In the closing, the writer invites others to read this book.

If you like tales of danger, mystery, and suspense wrapped into a story about courage, The True Confessions of Charlotte Doyle will keep you reading far into the night.

# Writing in a Reader Response Journal

A **reader response journal** is a notebook or journal in which you write freely about the books you read. In one writing, you may write about why you think the main character acts in a certain way. In a second writing, you may try to guess what will happen next in the story. In still another writing, you may relate some part of the story to your own life. The choice is yours.

## How to Respond

A response journal is very much like any other type of personal journal. You turn to it whenever you feel like writing about something you have read. The point is to make discoveries for yourself, so write as openly and honestly as you can. *Some of the ideas in your journal will help you write book reviews.*

## Ideas for Responding

For novels and other longer books, try to write in your journal at least four or five times. The following ideas will help you write responses at different points in your reading.

**First Feelings** ● What did you like about the opening chapter or two? How do you feel about the characters?

**On Your Way** ● Are the events in the reading clear to you? How do you feel about the characters and story now? What do you think will happen next?

**The Second Half** ● What seems important now? What questions or concerns do you have? Does the book keep your interest? Why or why not?

**Summing Up** ● How do you feel about the ending? How has the main character changed? How have you changed? What do you like most or least about this book and why?

**Bright IDEA**

**Here are some more ideas to try:** Carry on a conversation with a character, express your feelings in a poem, draw a picture, or try adding to or changing the story.

# Writing Explanations

## Recipe for a Baseball Card Collection
### by James Lambert

First, place the autographed Mickey Mantle rookie card in a 3" x 6" plastic pallet. Then, neatly arrange your complete set of Upper Deck cards with the Juan Gonzalez card on top. Next, make sure that the Cal Ripken card is separated from the other cards (otherwise, you'll never find it). Finally, place all of these hot cards on a shelf to cool, and check them from time to time.

## How to Do Something

While this set of directions is obviously not real, there are times when you really do have to explain things. For example, you might be asked to explain how to do something, how something works, or how to get from one place to the other. On the next three pages, you will find helpful guidelines and models for this form of writing.

# Writing an Explanation

**PREWRITING**  *Planning Your Writing*

**Select a Subject** ● Think of something you know how to do or make, or some skill you are interested in learning about. You may be skilled at shooting free throws, making pancakes, or *eating* pancakes.  Or you may be interested in exploring caves, buying a guitar, or starting a fan club.

**List the Steps** ● List the steps involved in completing your skill.  Or learn as much as you can about a new skill through reading, observing, interviewing, and participating.

## WRITING THE FIRST DRAFT

**Explain It Clearly** ● Explain how to carry out your skill from start to finish.  Start your explanation with a topic sentence that identifies the subject.

Helpful    Use linking words like *first, second, next,* and *then* to
Hint    help readers move from one step to the next.

**REVISING**  *Improving Your Writing*

**Test It Out** ● Carefully reread your first draft, making sure the directions are clear and complete.  If possible, have someone else try to do what you've explained by following your directions. This will help you see if you have missed any important points.

## EDITING & PROOFREADING

**Check It Out** ● Make sure that the revised draft of your writing reads smoothly and is free of careless errors.  Proofread the final copy before sharing it.

## Student Models

**How to Make Something** ● Here are the steps to a real recipe, stated very carefully and clearly.

### My Favorite Food
#### by Kimberly Tso

This is how my grandma makes fried bread. First she puts some flour in a bowl. She puts baking soda and salt with the flour. She gets some warm water. She puts in a little bit of water at a time while mixing the flour to make a dough. She kneads the dough to make it soft. Then she covers it with a cloth. She lets it set for 5 minutes. She puts a pan on the stove with grease in it. She waits until the grease gets hot. By that time the dough is ready. Then she starts making fried bread. She fries pieces of bread until they are golden brown, and they taste really good.

**How Something Works** ● The following model explains how the digestive system works.

### Digestion
#### by Lauren A. Kitchell

The digestive system is really a cycle. It starts as soon as you put food in your mouth. The food gets chewed up by the teeth. Then the salivary glands make a digestive juice called saliva. The saliva covers the chewed-up food, and the food goes down the esophagus or throat to the stomach. In the stomach the food gets churned up and covered with some more digestive juices. After the stomach does its job, the liver and pancreas add digestive juices for use in the small intestine. From the small intestine the digested food passes into the bloodstream. The wastes of the digested food go into the large intestine. In the large intestine the waste is stored and then finally goes out of the body.

**How to Get Someplace** ● In the following model, Hillary Bachman provides directions for the driver of a stretch limo that took Hillary and her friends on a special birthday ride.

### Birthday Ride

For my birthday ride, I want to go from my house to Chi-Chi's restaurant in La Crosse following this route. First, drive north four blocks until you reach Montgomery Street. Then take a left. Continue past the senior high and take the second left after you pass the school. This road will take you in a big loop back to where you first turned. After you pass the senior high again, turn right and drive past Lawrence Lawson Elementary School. Then take the second left. Drive until you reach Water Street and take a right. This will take you through downtown and past Tim's house (please honk) right after you pass the Morrow Home. Turn right when you come to the A & W. This highway (16) will take us directly to Chi-Chi's. Thank you!

**How to Create a Feeling** ● You can also use your imagination with explanations that create a feeling or a mood.

### Recipe for a Cozy Winter Day

1 snow-filled evergreen forest
1 small one-room log cabin
4 good friends who know lots of songs
1 blazing fireplace
4 mugs of hot chocolate
1 plate of chocolate chip cookies
4 marshmallows

Directions: Take small one-room log cabin. Place it in the middle of a snow-filled evergreen forest. Fill the cabin with four good friends in front of a blazing fireplace. Serve each friend a mug of hot chocolate. Put one marshmallow into each mug. Pass around one plate piled high with chocolate chip cookies. Mix in singing voices, and your cozy winter day will be complete.

# Writing Business Letters

## When You Mean Business

A **business letter** is different from a letter you write to an aunt in another city or to a pen pal in another country. It looks and sounds more business-like and focuses on only one subject.

You may write a business letter for different reasons:

- **when you need information** (*a letter of request*),

- **when you have a problem with something you ordered** (*a letter of complaint*),

- **or when you have a problem with a situation in your city or school** (*a letter to an editor or official*).

But no matter what type of business letter you write, you should follow the guidelines given in this chapter. Your letters will bring better results if you do them right. Pay special attention to the sample letter on page 145.

# Types of Business Letters

There are three types of business letters described below: **a letter of request**, **a letter of complaint**, and **a letter to an editor or official**.

### Letter of Request ● You want to go to Yellowstone

National Park on your vacation next summer, but you need to convince the rest of the family. You decide to write a letter of request asking for information. Here are some guidelines you could use. (**SEE** the model on page 145.)

✔ Explain why you are writing.

✔ Ask any questions you have.

✔ Describe what you would like to receive (and when).

✔ Thank them for their help.

### Letter of Complaint ● You ordered a pair of high-tops

and received two left shoes. How will you get the shoes exchanged or ask for your money back? You could write a letter of complaint.

✔ Describe the product.

✔ Describe the problem and possible causes.

✔ Explain how you have tried to solve the problem.

✔ End with what you would like the reader (or company) to do.

### Letter to an Editor or Official ● The traffic on your

street makes it dangerous for children. How will you get the city to do something about the situation? You could write a letter to your local newspaper, or to a public official. (**SEE** page 131 for a model.)

✔ Describe the situation.

✔ Tell what you think about the situation.

✔ If you have ideas for improvement or change, explain them.

✔ Support your ideas with facts and examples.

✔ End by asking that the situation be changed.

# Parts of a Business Letter

**Heading** ● The **heading** includes the sender's address and date. Write the heading about an inch from the top of the page at the left-hand margin.

**Inside Address** ● The **inside address** includes the name and address of the person or company you are writing to. Place it at the left-hand margin, four to seven spaces below the heading. If the person has a special title such as park ranger, add it after his or her name. (Use a comma first.)

**Mr. David Shore, Park Ranger**

**Salutation** ● The **salutation** is a greeting, a way of saying hello. Write it on the second line below the inside address. Always use a colon at the end of the salutation.

➤ If you know the person's name, write:

**Dear Mr. Shore:**

➤ If you don't know the person's name, write:

**Dear Park Ranger:**

**Dear Sir or Madam:**

**Dear Yellowstone Park:**

**Greetings:**

**Body** ● The **body** is the main part of the letter. Begin this part two lines below the salutation. Double-space between each paragraph. Do not indent. Keep the information brief and simple so the reader clearly understands what you are asking for or explaining.

**Closing** ● Place the **closing** at the left-hand margin, two spaces below the body. Use **Very truly**, **Yours truly**, or **Sincerely** for a business letter closing. Capitalize the first word but not the others. Always place a comma after the closing.

**Signature** ● End your letter by signing your name beneath the closing. If you are typing your letter, skip four lines and type your full name. Then write your **signature** between the closing and your typed name.

## Sample Business Letter

**Heading**

4824 Park Street
Richland Center, WI  53581
January 1, 1994

**Inside Address**

Mr. David Shore, Park Ranger
Yellowstone National Park
Box 168
Yellowstone National Park, WY  82190

**Salutation**

Dear Mr. Shore:

We're having a contest in my family to see
who can plan the best summer vacation.  I
want to convince everyone that a trip to
Yellowstone National Park would be better
than going to New York City or even to
Disneyland for a week.  This is not going to
be easy!

**Body**

I would appreciate any help you could give
me.  I am most interested in some up-to-date
brochures of the park with photos and maps.
I will also need information on where we can
stay and what we can do there.

Thank you for your help.  Maybe I'll see you
next summer.

**Closing**

Sincerely,

*Luke Johnson*

**Signature**

Luke Johnson

# Folding Your Letter

When you finish your letter, fold it in three parts.

*Like this:*    ■ Fold bottom one-third up.
           ■ Next, fold top one-third down.
           ■ Crease the folds firmly.
           ■ Insert into envelope.

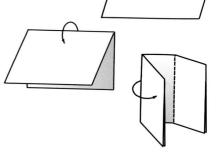

*Or like this:*    ■ Fold letter in half.
            ■ Next, fold into thirds.
            ■ Crease folds firmly.
            ■ Insert into envelope.

# Sending Your Letter

## Address the Envelope

- Place the full name and complete address of the person to whom the letter is being sent slightly to the left of the middle of the envelope.

- Place your return address in the upper left-hand corner of the envelope and the stamp in the upper right-hand corner.

```
MR LUKE JOHNSON
4824 PARK ST
RICHLAND CENTER  WI  53581
```

```
          MR DAVID SHORE
          PARK RANGER
          YELLOWSTONE NATIONAL PARK
          BOX 168
          YELLOWSTONE NATIONAL PARK  WY  82190
```

When addressing your envelope, the post office prefers that you use all capital letters, no punctuation, and the two-letter abbreviations for states. (**SEE** page 357 for a list of abbreviations.)

# Writing a Business Letter

**PREWRITING** *Planning Your Letter*

✔ Check your handbook for the requirements for the different types of business letters: **Letter of Request**, **Letter to an Editor or Official**, **Letter of Complaint**.

✔ Gather all of the details and facts you need.

✔ Organize your ideas for your writing.

**WRITING THE FIRST DRAFT**

✔ Write naturally, but keep the style somewhat formal.

✔ Explain your main points clearly.

✔ Write short paragraphs.

**REVISING** *Improving Your Writing*

✔ Make sure you have included the necessary facts and details.

✔ Make sure you have written honestly and sincerely.

✔ Make sure your letter is easy to read.

**EDITING & PROOFREADING**

✔ Make sure you proofread for punctuation, capitalization, and grammar errors. (Pay special attention to the heading, inside address, and salutation.)

✔ Make sure you've included all the necessary "parts" of a business letter. (**SEE** page 144.)

✔ Make sure your letter is neatly written or typed.

✔ Center the letter and keep the margins even.

✔ Use only one side of the paper.

# Writing Observation Reports

I hear kids shouting. There is a strange scent in the air. There is a faint breeze. It is 9:35 Saturday morning, and the playground is filling up with kids. Cars keep whizzing past. Suddenly a rollerblader zooms by . . .

## Using Your Senses

You have just read part of an observation report. The subject is a playground where the writer observes different *sights, sounds, smells,* and *physical feelings.* In other words, all of the writer's senses are focused on his subject. In an observation report, there is no need to get involved in any action. You simply select a location and look, listen, and learn.

# Writing an Observation Report

**PREWRITING**   *Planning Your Writing*

**Select a Location** ● Observe a room in your school, a street corner, a bus or subway car, a small store, an entrance to a mall, a kitchen.  The choice is yours.

**Observe and Write** ● In a notebook, write down what you see, hear, smell, and feel at this location.  If there is a lot of activity, take quick notes so you don't miss anything.  (Spend at least 15 minutes at this location.)

 You may find a camcorder helpful for collecting, but check with your teacher before you do any recording.

## WRITING THE FIRST DRAFT

**Prepare Your Report** ● You can write your observation report in two different ways.

**1** You can share all of the details in the order that you listed them.  In this way, your report will flow from one sight or sound to another.  This is how the model at the beginning of the chapter is written.

**2** You can organize your observations around a main idea just as you would in a descriptive paragraph.  (See the model on the next page.)

**REVISING & EDITING**   *Improving Your Writing*

**Decide What Changes Need to Be Made** ● Review your first draft once to make sure that it contains all of the important observations (sights and sounds).  Review it a second time to check for sentence, spelling, and punctuation errors.  Make all of the needed changes; then proofread the final draft of your report.

## Model Observation Report

The main idea in this model paragraph is stated in the first sentence. All of the observations that follow relate to this idea.

### The Big Chill
by Todd Michael

As we wait for the Christmas parade, everyone looks cold. My little brother sits on my mom's lap, trying to hide from the wind. The little boy and girl sitting next to my mom have snowsuits on, plus they have a green blanket wrapped around them. Two or three different times they say, "Mom, can we pleeease have some hot chocolate?" The man standing behind us says, "I'm from Charlotte, and I'm not used to the cold." I hear another voice say, "Just wait until it starts to snow." Five boys next to me are playing tackle tag to keep warm. They all wear colorful ski jackets and ear warmers. The road in front of us looks drab and gray under the streetlight. One family on the other curb is wrapped inside a big blue quilt. Just then a siren sounds. The parade is finally about to begin.

**THINK IT OVER**

Always try to show rather than tell in your writing. A *showing* sentence like "My little brother sits on my mom's lap, trying to hide from the wind" says much more than a *telling* sentence like "It was windy." (**SEE** "Show Don't Tell" on page 40 for more examples.)

## Science Observation Report

In your science class, you may be asked to write an observation report on an experiment or project. For one of his science projects, Emery Sanford observed how mold grows on different kinds of bread. Part of his final report follows.

### Observing Mold on Bread

**PROCEDURE:** On October 27, I brought my bread to school. I had four different kinds of bread: Clausen's white bread, Roman Meal bread, French bread, and pita bread. I put each piece of bread in a sandwich bag and waited a few days for the mold to grow.

**OBSERVATIONS:** The Clausen's bread started growing mold first. The mold was green and white. Before this, I had never seen anything other than green mold on bread. This was the first thing I learned about mold. . . .

The Roman Meal started by getting little white speckles on it. In four days there was mold on the bread. It got green, white, and yellow mold at first. Now I had found yellow mold. I had seen two new colors that I had never seen before. . . .

The French bread got stale very quickly. It got very hard and then it started getting moldy. The mold grew on the inside of the bread, not on the outside like the others.

The pita didn't grow mold at all, probably because it is made from whole wheat and oat bran. It did get hard. That's something I didn't know, that pita bread can get stale, but not moldy.

**CONCLUSIONS:** I learned a lot of things during this observation. I learned that there are different colored molds, why the bread shrinks (which took some thinking), how mold grows, what mold looks like under a microscope, and how it forms. And most important, I learned what kind of bread to buy if you want it to last: either pita or Roman Meal.

# Writing Tales and Stories

**Writing Fantasies**

**Writing Tall Tales**

**Writing Realistic Stories**

**Writing Stories from History**

# Writing Fantasies

## Inventing Impossible Things

Do you ever daydream? Have you ever had an imaginary friend? Have you ever made believe you could fly, or wished you were an explorer? Have you ever invented your own private world, or pretended to be one of the characters in your favorite book? If so, you've been using your imagination, and when you do that, *anything* can happen—even impossible things.

**66** *When you write a story, you can imagine it any way you want, just as long as your readers believe you.* **99**
— *Nancy Bond*

## Animals That Talk?

Anytime you write stories, you use your imagination. In one special kind of story, you get to make up all the rules yourself. It's called *fantasy*, the type of story where even a spider can save a pig. So let's begin by reading a fantasy story by a student writer.

## Student Model

In this story, a girl named Penny and her barnyard friends try to figure out why Montgomery the cat is acting so strangely.

The setting is described in the opening paragraph.

### MONTGOMERY MEWS MYSTERIOUSLY
#### by Katie Ambrogi

There was a dusty barn made of old gray wood. The nails marked their age with signs of permanent rust. An old silo stood next to the barn. It looked queer and was every bit as old as the barn.

Just then, Penny appeared in front of the barn. The animals looked up at her in surprise. Penny never came into the barnyard at this time of day!

"I insist on a barnyard meeting, now!" declared Penny.

Sandy the pig stopped rolling in the mud. Mr. Winkle, otherwise known as Perry the rooster, stopped stalking the barnyard. Freedom the dog stopped lapping up week-old water. Oxford, the biggest ox you've ever seen, let out a great big bellow from the barn.

Baanie the sheep said to Penny, "What's the matter?"

"Yeah, what's wrong?" chorused all the animals.

"Have any of you seen Montgomery?" Penny inquired.

"No," chorused the animals.

"Well, neither have I, and I'm beginning to worry. She's hardly ever around," said Penny.

"Well," began Oxford, who was always a close observer, "Montgomery looked different today in a way I can't put my finger on, but she was very nice to Sandy. That's a sure sign that something is wrong."

"Mr. Winkle, do you think we should pry into the cat's business?" Freedom asked.

Then the characters and their problem are identified.

Sandy, who was listening to the conversation, stepped in and said, "No . . . but there could be something wrong with Montgomery. Not that I really care."

"Okay," began Oxford, "here's the deal. Winkle, you are the chief administrator of the spy office. We will run around, watch Montgomery closely, and report our messages to the office."

"What about me?" asked Penny.

"Penny, you record everything the spies report," Mr. Winkle said.

Just then, Montgomery slid into the barn. "Why is everyone staring at me like that? I'm fine." Montgomery quickly turned around and made her way out of the barn.

Hours later, they still had no clue to what was wrong with Montgomery. Sandy sat at her desk and tapped her fingers. Mr. Winkle fluffed up his feathers and started to twiddle his thumbs. Penny jotted down reports, but nothing was good enough to lead them to an answer.

Then the barnyard door swung open a crack. Montgomery slid through it. Six pairs of eyes traveled to the door. "You know," Montgomery began, "I guess I should have told you." The animals listened in suspense.

"You know how cats love privacy," Montgomery started again. Just then, two kittens timidly stepped in. "They were born three weeks ago," Montgomery said, her voice full of pride. She introduced the kittens. "The little one I call Mouse . . ."

So, somewhere in a barn in Vermont, there are six happy barnyard adults, two happy kittens, and one happy girl.

The characters decide how they will deal with their problem.

After hours of suspense, the problem is solved.

# One Writer's Process

When I write a fantasy, I want to make my readers *believe* my story. I want them to think it could happen, just the way I've imagined it. I want them willing to pretend with me. Here's how I usually get started on my stories.

## ➤ Keep a Writer's Notebook

Ideas can come from anywhere at any time. I find it helps to write them down before I forget them. I can't use everything I put in my notebook, but sometimes just writing down a word or two can start a story growing in my imagination. I write down anything that interests me: funny names, unusual objects, silly thoughts. Then when I need an idea, I can look back and see what I've got.

## ➤ Ask Questions

When I write a story, I ask myself lots of questions about what's going on. I'll show you what I mean. Almost everyone's imagined what it would be like to fly like a bird. Suppose we want to write a story about a girl who can really do it. To me, the most interesting thing is not so much that she can fly. I want to know how she does it and what it feels like.

## ➤ Make Choices

The first thing we have to do is get the girl into the air. But how? Have you ever seen a Canada goose take off from a pond or a riverbank? Maybe *that's* how she does it, by running faster and faster and flapping her arms.

Maybe she flies by concentrating on feeling light. Or perhaps she has to think of nothing at all. Remember Peter Pan? He told Wendy, John, and Michael to "think lovely thoughts, and up you go!" That's another way. Have you got other ideas?

## ➤ Ask More Questions

Let's go a little further. Now our girl is in the air, however we decided to get her there. Let's ask some more questions. How does it feel? Does she ride the wind like a kite? Or does she have to keep flapping her arms like a bird? When she's up in the sky, what do the clouds feel like? Are they wet and cold, or soft and warm like down comforters? Maybe they're sticky, like cotton candy.

## ➤ Start the Story

To describe this girl in action and build some excitement into my story, I might write something like this:

> Cynthia had no warning. One minute there she was, floating on soft pillows of warm air. Her wings were stretched wide while she admired her neighborhood. Here and there among the trees a swimming pool glinted at her, a miniature car winked in the sun, and tiny people followed sidewalks, never thinking to look up to see Cynthia Bean gliding over their heads.
>
> Suddenly she blinked. It was all gone: the sun, the warmth, the houses on her block. Gray blankness filled her eyes. In a blind panic, she curled into a ball, hugging her wings tight around her, and dropped like a stone out through the bottom of the cloud . . .

Why was Cynthia falling? What will happen to her? How could this action lead to other exciting events? I would try to answer these questions as I wrote the rest of my fantasy.

**THINK IT OVER**

Can you think of someone else who might fly into a story? How about a young boy who suddenly finds himself floating in air on his way home from school? Why is he floating? What will he do about it?

# Writing a Fantasy

## PREWRITING *Planning Your Story*

**Invent Characters** ● Fantasy characters can be real people, talking animals, dragons, unicorns, or creatures you invent yourself. (Think of a main character and maybe one or two others.)

What are your characters' names? What do they look like? What do they like to do? Write about them and find out.

**Choose a Problem to Solve** ● In a fantasy, the main character's problem may be finding out why a cat is acting strangely, searching for a treasure, finding the way back home, and so on. (The way your main character solves his or her problem is the plot, the main part of your story.)

**Find a Setting** ● Fantasy can take place anywhere or anytime—in your neighborhood or a magical place. (Describe the setting so that your readers can see it in their minds.)

## WRITING THE FIRST DRAFT

**Get Started** ● Begin your story by introducing the main character or setting. Or begin with something happening like two characters arguing, a narrow escape, an explosion, and so on. This action should lead to the main problem in the story.

**Keep It Going** ● As you continue, try to make the main character's life more and more difficult because of the problem. Include lots of dialogue. This will keep your readers interested.

**Stop When You Get to the End** ● The end of the story comes when the problem is solved. That sounds obvious, but sometimes writers go on to explain what their stories are about and end up writing too much.

## REVISING    *Improving Your Writing*

**Let It Sit** ● After you've written your story, let it sit for a while. Then, when you read it again, try pretending someone else wrote it, and see what you think. You'll never be able to fool yourself totally, but you'll be able to see it a little more clearly.

**Make It Believable** ● Remember that your story should be imaginary *and* believable. Ask, "Do my characters act in a way that fits the story? Do the actions make sense in my setting?"

**Share Your First Draft** ● Listen carefully to the questions your friends ask after reading or listening to your story. This can be hard to do, but when you write a story for other people, you want them to understand it. One of your friends may be confused by something you have said in the introduction. Another friend may think that a part of your story isn't believable.

 If you're not sure about your story's ending, try removing the last sentence or paragraph. See if the story seems complete without it.

## EDITING & PROOFREADING

**Edit** ● Take a close look at the specific words and sentences in your story once you have made all of the major changes. Have you picked the best words to describe the setting, characters, and action? Are your sentences interesting and clear? Have you used enough dialogue and punctuated it correctly?

**Proofread** ● Also make sure to proofread the final draft of your story before you share it.

 Writing fantasies can be fun, but reading them can be even more enjoyable. Have you read these popular fantasies?
- *A String in the Harp* by Nancy Bond
- *Flat Stanley* by Jeff Brown
- *A Wrinkle in Time* by Madeleine L'Engle

# Writing Tall Tales

## Ride That Mosquito!

Throughout history, **tall tales** have been told by people struggling to survive. These tales contain extraordinary heroes and heroines who can defeat anything and anybody. And they are filled with humor and exaggeration:

*Daniel Boone told of smacking a mosquito with the flat of his hatchet "to calm it down a bit." Then he put a saddle on that mosquito and rode it.*

People still enjoy inventing tall tales. When you use language like "she was so mean" or "he was so strong," you are well on your way to inventing a tall tale.

> **66** For tall tales, ordinary, run-of-the-mill, polite little lies won't do, no siree. Tall tales need lies so big and exaggerated that they make you laugh out loud and beg for more. **99**
> —Susan Ohanian

## Model Tall Tale

In the following tall tale, Big Bob is faced with a big problem: he has to catch a runaway state!

Big Bob is described using exaggeration.

The hero has a powerful force to overcome.

He uses his strength and craftiness to tame Texas.

### BIG BOB AND THE MISSING STATE
#### by Christopher Meyer

Dear Bob,

Knowing you are as fast as lightning with a lasso, I thought you might be able to complete this mission. Last night the chains broke loose and Texas ran away. We need you to catch it and bring it back. Good luck.

Mr. President

Texas was the fastest state in the world, but that didn't worry Bob. The next morning Bob got up, got dressed, got out his biggest lasso, which could wrap around the moon, got on his horse, and off he went to catch Texas. He rode through Utah, Nevada, Colorado, and California, but he didn't find Texas. Then one day while he was riding through Mexico, he heard a distant rumble. He started riding that way. Sure enough, when he got there, he found Texas running full speed away from him. He got off his horse and threw his lasso as hard as he could until it was out of sight. Then he lay down for the night.

The next morning he got up and ate breakfast. All of a sudden his lasso pulled tight and he knew he had lassoed Texas. He pulled and pulled and dragged it back to its place and chained it down tight so it wouldn't get away again.

# Writing a Tall Tale

**PREWRITING** *Planning Your Story*

You can build your own tall tales by following these guidelines:

**Choose a Hero or Heroine** ● Remember that these heroes are always strong, brave, and smart. Use exaggeration when you describe this person. Your hero or heroine may be

    . . . as strong as the Sahara Desert is dry.

    . . . as smart as a city full of brain surgeons.

**Create a Powerful Foe** ● Think of a powerful foe or force that your hero must tame. This foe may be

    . . . an outlaw so mean he could scare an entire army.

    . . . a winter so cold that even the antifreeze freezes.

    . . . a mosquito so big it needs a runway to land.

**Show the Cleverness of Your Hero** ● To tame or escape the powerful foe, your hero or heroine may be able to

    . . . outsnarl and outsnort a grizzly bear.

    . . . wrap a lasso around a runaway state.

## A Tall Cast of Characters

Knowing something about four famous tall-tale heroes may help you plan your own story:

● *Sally Ann Thunder Ann Whirlwind Crockett uses her bowie knife as a toothpick and skins a bear faster than an alligator swallows a fish.*

● *Mighty medicine man Glooskap squeezes a water monster whose warts are as big as mountains until the monster becomes a mere bullfrog.*

● *Pecos Bill ties rattlesnakes together and invents the clothesline.*

● *Old Sally Cato crawls into the belly of the giant Billy Bally Bully and shakes out clouds of dust to make the giant wheeze and sneeze.*

## WRITING YOUR STORY

Tall tales are meant to be fun and entertaining. So remember to include a lot of exaggeration and humor in your writing. If you use dialogue, have the main character say things that are funny or clever, and have other characters say things that sound a little silly or simple. (More writing tips are provided below.)

Think of yourself as an old-time storyteller with a group of eager listeners around you. Your job is to tell them a good story.

**Start Out Creatively** ● Introduce the main character in a creative way. (In the model, Big Bob is introduced in a letter written by the president.) Also introduce the foe your hero will be up against. Remember to exaggerate!

**Keep It Going** ● Have your main character set out to tame the foe. Try not to make things too easy for your hero. He or she may have to do some searching, fighting, building, waiting, and so on.

**End Your Story** ● In a tall tale, the main character almost always wins in the end. Will your hero win because of her or his strength, craftiness, or a combination of the two? Will there be any surprises at the end of your story?

Reading different types of tall tales will give you new ideas for your own writing. Here are three titles to consider:

- *Sally Ann Thunder Ann Whirlwind Crockett* by Caron Lee Cohen
- *How Glooskap Outwits the Ice Giant and Other Tales of the Maritime Indians* by Howard Norman
- *Cut From the Same Cloth: American Women of Myth, Legend, and Tall Tale* by Robert San Souci

# Writing Realistic Stories

## Amanda Comes to Life

Amanda Lowe is 11 years old. She attends Peabody Elementary School in Philadelphia. Her long red hair curls wildly, like fire flaming out of control. She is the shortest student in sixth grade.

Amanda hates being short. And she wishes she could be brave enough to tell everyone to stop treating her like somebody's kid sister. But what would happen if she did? Amanda isn't sure she wants to find out.

## What are realistic stories?

*Ideas for realistic stories often come from a writer's own experiences or interests. But the finished products are more fiction (made-up) than fact.*

What I have just described is an idea for a **realistic story**. The main character in a realistic story may remind you of someone you know. For instance, you may know someone like Amanda. Her problem (being too short) may sound very believable. But a realistic story has not actually happened. It only *seems* real.

## Planning Guide

To help you keep track of all of your planning ideas, you may want to use a "Collection Sheet" like the one below. You don't have to fill in all of the information before you write, and you should feel free to make changes at any time. (Sometimes a sheet like this is very helpful *after* you write your first draft. It helps you see if you have covered all of the basics in your story.)

# Collection Sheet

*Characters:*

(List the main character first. How old are your characters and what will their names be? Think how each of your characters might look, speak, and act.)

*Setting:*

(Describe where and when the story will take place.)

*Problem:*

(What problem does the main character need to solve?)

*Story Scenes:*

(What are some of the things your main character may try in order to solve her or his problem?)

*Purpose:*

(Will your story be serious, surprising, scary, funny, or sad? One of these feelings can be a guide for your writing.)

**TALK About It**

Talk about your story ideas with your classmates before (and after) you write your first draft. As you discuss your story, at least one or two more ideas will pop into your mind.

## WRITING THE FIRST DRAFT

Most writers would tell you to begin your story right in the middle of the action, but you may start your story any way you want to. Start with "One day last summer . . ." if that feels right to you. (You can always change it later on.)

**Start Your Story** ● Here are five ways to begin a story.

■ Begin with dialogue:
> *"Put me down!" Amanda shouted.*

■ Begin with a question:
> *How did this super athlete get stuck in such a small body?*

■ Begin with description:
> *The gym smelled like sweat and stale popcorn.*

■ Begin with background information:
> *All through elementary school, Amanda*
> *had been treated like a kid sister.*

■ Begin with the main character introducing herself:
> *I might as well tell you now and get it over with.*
> *I am the shortest person in sixth grade.*

**Keep Your Story Going** ● Try not to make things too easy for your character. You may have her involved in two or three important actions because of her problem. She may do some talking, thinking, running, fighting, and so on.

**End Your Story** ● Your story does not have to end on a happy note. Some problems just can't be solved or completely overcome. For example, Amanda Lowe can't make herself grow taller, no matter how many bowls of Wheaties she eats. But she may be able to get her classmates to treat her with more respect.

Most characters change in some way because of their problems. That's something to keep in mind as you write your story.

## REVISING   *Improving Your Story*

As you review your first draft, make sure that all of the characters' words and actions make sense. Also make sure that your story does not move along too quickly or too slowly. The key is to keep your readers interested.

**Add Life to Your Story** ● If your story needs to be pumped up, try adding more details, dialogue, and action.

■ Use specific details:

> *Are there any sights, sounds, smells, and feelings that you could add? Have you described the characters and the setting in your story?*

■ Use dialogue and action:

> *Would you like your story to be more active? Then include more dialogue and action scenes. Notice how the special combination of the two can build excitement:*

*"Put me down!" Amanda shouted.*
*"Make me!" Eric dared.*
*"Okay, you asked for it!"*
*Amanda twisted and kicked until Eric lost his grip. As she fell, she grabbed hold of his hair . . . .*

## EDITING & PROOFREADING

Once you have made all of the major changes in your story, read it again to make sure that it reads smoothly and clearly from start to finish. Also check your work for punctuation, spelling, and grammar errors. (Ask a trusted friend or classmate to help you.) Then complete a neat final draft of your story. Proofread this copy before you share it.

# Writing Stories from History

## Long Ago and Far Away . . .

- *Would you like to go back in time?*
- *Would you like to meet someone from the past?*
- *Would you like to relive a great event?*

You can do all of these things by writing historical stories, stories based on what *could* have happened or what *did* happen at a certain time or place. What's so exciting about this type of writing is that there is so much history to choose from.

A historical story should be part fact and part fiction and believable all the way through.

# Writing a Historical Story

**PREWRITING** *Planning Your Story*

**Think Historically** ● When you plan and write a historical story, you may choose a historical period or event and make up characters that could have lived during that time. Or you may choose someone real, making this person your main character.

**List Ideas** ● The first thing you should do is make a list of different *times, events,* or *people* from history that you might like to write about. For ideas, think of history units you have studied in class and different times and people that you have always been interested in. The sample ideas that follow will help you get started.  (Try to list at least five ideas of your own.)

- **Massasoit and the first Thanksgiving** (*an event*)
- **Middle Ages in Europe** (*a historical time*)
- **The Oregon Trail** (*a historical place*)
- **Ferdinand Magellan** (*a famous explorer*)
- **Harriet Tubman** (*a famous freedom fighter*)

**Select a Subject** ● Once you complete your list, put a check next to the idea that interests you the most.  Use this idea as the starting point for your story research.  (If you find that one idea doesn't work out so well, you can always try another from your list.)

**WRITE** About It   Write freely for 3 to 5 minutes about your subject to help you see what you already know, and what you may need to find out.

**Collect Facts** ● To collect new information about your subject, start by reading about it in an encyclopedia article, in another basic reference book, or in your history text. Ask your teacher or librarian about other sources of information, too. Take careful notes as you read. (See the sample notes below.)

## Sample Note-Taking Page

Listed here are facts that could have been collected for a historical story on the voyage of Ferdinand Magellan.

### Facts About Ferdinand Magellan

- a Portuguese sailor who planned to sail around the world
- began his voyage on Sept. 20, 1519
- hardships began immediately (several mutinies)
- ran out of food; crew ate rats and ox hides
- stopped at the Philippines for food
- April 27, 1521, Magellan killed during a battle on the island of Mactan
- of the original 241 sailors only 110 remained
- Trinidad didn't make it back, sailors imprisoned
- Victoria under command of Juan Sebastian del Cano returned to Spain on Sept. 6, 1522
- only Juan Sebastian del Cano and 17 others survived
- Italian crew member Antonio Pigafetta kept a journal

You might find it easier to collect information by starting with a series of basic questions: *Where did Magellan's men sail? Why were they sailing? What happened to them?*

**Identify Your Story Elements** ● Continue your planning by identifying the basic elements for your story. You may want to use a "Collection Sheet" to help you keep track of your ideas. Use your collection sheet as you write, but feel free to make changes at any time as you go along.

# Collection Sheet

*Characters:*

(Decide how each of your characters might look, speak, and act. Remember to keep the time period of your story in mind.)

*Setting:*

(Describe the historical time and place of your story.)

*Main Action:*

(What action will your character be involved in? This action may or may not be true. But it must be believable. Within this main action, there may be some type of problem that needs to be solved.)

*Story Scenes:*

(What are some of the things your character might do—fighting, planning, eating, etc.—during the main action?)

*Form:*

(Decide what form your story will take. You may write a basic story, or you may choose another form—a diary or a series of letters. The model on page 175 is told in diary form.)

## WRITING THE FIRST DRAFT

**Begin Your Story** ● Start your story with some dialogue, an action scene, or a brief description. Work in background facts and introduce the main characters as soon as possible.

> *"Get down, Antonio. They will see you. Get down."*
> *Everything was happening so fast. Captain Magellan was dead, the crew had scattered into the woods, and now we were under attack.*
> *"Juan," whispered Antonio. "Since the captain is dead, you are now in charge. You must get us out of here. You must."*
> *Yes, Antonio was right. I, Juan Sebastian del Cano, was in charge. But get us out of here? How?*

**Keep Your Story Going** ● Remember that your story should be based on historical fact, and it should seem realistic. Keep these points in mind as your main character gets more involved in the story.

**End Your Story** ● Don't drag your story out. It should end when the main action is completed. Remember, too, that your story does not have to end on a happy note.

## REVISING & EDITING *A Final Checklist*

✔ Do all of the characters' words and actions make sense, considering the historical time? (George Washington wouldn't say something like, "Don't get hyper!")

✔ Does the story build in interest? (Does the main character complete the action or solve the problem in the story?)

✔ Do your sentences read smoothly? (Let a friend read it to you.)

✔ Is your final draft neat and easy to read?

## Student Model

Heather Stoll's story is about a baker who lived during the Middle Ages. The story is told in the form of a diary. The introduction and two entries from the diary are shown below:

*Here, you will see Genoa, Italy, through the eyes of Piero Baker, a well-to-do baker and pastry maker. Piero's shop is on Mill Road. He is a member of the guild of pastry makers. In his diary, you will find information about different shops, clothes, and products related to the Middle Ages.*

# Genoa, Italy, in the Middle Ages

## September 3, 1348

Today I acquired four bags of flour in return for baking two loaves of bread for Widow Napoli.

Dominic and I finished Lady Sophia's order of trenchers today. She paid me well: ten bags of flour, fourteen gold coins, one yard of silk.

My wife will be pleased to see the latter. She has been awanting for a new dress.

Today I must go to the woods and cut myself a new oven spatula. Mine is sorely burnt and in need of repairs.

## September 17, 1348

That clumsy excuse for a helper, Fos, spilled flour all over the floor! Now precious time must be wasted cleaning up.

The order is now more than half done. Lady Sophia is relieved. Already she is hiring minstrels and dancers, and the hall bustles with activity.

Everyone is excited! The fleet must be almost ready to go. They leave tomorrow. It is five days' voyage from the boot of my dear country to Genoa.

# Writing Poems, Plays, and Songs

**Writing Poems**

**Writing Songs**

**Writing Plays**

**Writing Riddles**

**Writing for Fun**